SHEPHERD'S NOTES

Shepherd's Notes Titles Available

SHEPHERD'S NOTES COMMENTARY SERIES

Old Testament

0-80549-028-0	Genesis	0-80549-341-7	Psalms 101-150
0-80549-056-6	Exodus	0-80549-016-7	Proverbs
0-80549-069-8	Leviticus & Numbers	0-80549-059-0	Ecclesiastes, Song of
0-80549-027-2	Deuteronomy		Solomon
0-80549-058-2	Joshua & Judges	0-80549-197-X	Isaiah
0-80549-057-4	Ruth & Esther	0-80549-070-1	Jeremiah-
0-80549-063-9	1 & 2 Samuel		Lamentations
0-80549-007-8	1 & 2 Kings	0-80549-078-7	Ezekiel
0-80549-064-7	1 & 2 Chronicles	0-80549-015-9	Daniel
0-80549-194-5	Ezra, Nehemiah	0-80549-326-3	Hosea-Obadiah
0-80549-006-X	Job	0-80549-334-4	Jonah-Zephaniah
0-80549-339-5	Psalms 1-50	0-80549-065-5	Haggai-Malachi
0-80549-340-9	Psalms 51-100		

New Testament

1-55819-688-9	Matthew	1-55819-689-7	Philippians,
0-80549-071-X	Mark		Colossians, &
0-80549-004-3	Luke		Philemon
1-55819-693-5	John	0-80549-000-0	1 & 2 Thessalonians
1-55819-691-9	Acts	1-55819-692-7	1 & 2 Timothy, Titus
0-80549-005-1	Romans	0-80549-336-0	Hebrews
0-80549-325-5	1 Corinthians	0-80549-018-3	James
0-80549-335-2	2 Corinthians	0-80549-019-1	1 & 2 Peter & Jude
1-55819-690-0	Galatians	0-80549-214-3	1, 2 & 3 John
0-80549-327-1	Ephesians	0-80549-017-5	Revelation

SHEPHERD'S NOTES CHRISTIAN CLASSICS

0-80549-347-6	Mere Christianity-C.S.Lewis	0-80549-394-8	Miracles-C.S.Lewis
0-80549-353-0	The Problem of Pain/ A Grief Observed-C.S.Lewis	0-80549-196-1	Lectures to My Students-Charles Haddon Spurgeon
0-80549-199-6	The Confessions-Augustine	0-80549-220-8	The Writings of Justin Martyr
0-80549-200-3	Calvin's Institutes	0-80549-345-X	The City of God

SHEPHERD'S NOTES-BIBLE SUMMARY SERIES

0-80549-377-8	Old Testament	0-80549-385-9	Life & Letters of Paul
0-80549-378-6	New Testament	0-80549-376-X	Manners & Customs of Bible Times
0-80549-384-0	Life & Teachings of Jesus	0-80549-380-8	Basic Christian Beliefs

SHEPHERD'S NOTES

When you need a guide through the Scriptures

I, II & III *John*

BROADMAN
&HOLMAN
PUBLISHERS

Nashville, Tennessee

Shepherd's Notes—*1,2,3 John*
© 1998
by Broadman & Holman Publishers
Nashville, Tennessee
All rights reserved
Printed in the United States of America

0–8054–9214–3
Dewey Decimal Classification: 227.9
Subject Heading: BIBLE. N.T. EPISTLES OF JOHN
Library of Congress Card Catalog Number: 98–15307

Library of Congress Cataloging-in-Publication Data

First, Second, and Third John / Rodney Combs, editor
   p. cm. — (Shepherd's notes)
  Includes bibliographical references.
  ISBN 0–8054–9214–3
  1. Bible. N.T. Epistles of John—Study and teaching. I. Combs, Rodney,
1965– . II. Series
 BS2805.5.F57 1998
 227'.94'007—dc21
              98–15307
                CIP

3 4 5 6 7 08 07 06 05

CONTENTS

Dear Reader:

Shepherd's Notes are designed to give you a quick, step-by-step overview of every book of the Bible. They are not meant to be substitutes for the biblical text; rather, they are study guides intended to help you explore the wisdom of Scripture in personal or group study and to apply that wisdom successfully in your own life.

Shepherd's Notes guide you through the main themes of each book of the Bible and illuminate fascinating details through appropriate commentary and reference notes. Historical and cultural background information brings the Bible into sharper focus.

Six different icons, used throughout the series, call your attention to historical-cultural information, Old Testament and New Testament references, word pictures, unit summaries, and personal application for everyday life.

Whether you are a novice or a veteran at Bible study, I believe you will find *Shepherd's Notes* a resource that will take you to a new level in your mining and applying the riches of Scripture.

In Him,

David R. Shepherd
Editor-in-Chief

DESIGNED FOR THE BUSY USER

Shepherd's Notes for 1,2,3 John is designed to provide an easy-to-use tool for getting a quick handle on this Bible book's important features, and for gaining an understanding of the message of 1,2,3 John. Information available in more difficult-to-use reference works has been incorporated into the *Shepherd's Notes* format. This brings you the benefits of many more advanced and expensive works packed into one small volume.

Shepherd's Notes are for laymen, pastors, teachers, small-group leaders and participants, as well as the classroom student. Enrich your personal study or quiet time. Shorten your class or small-group preparation time as you gain valuable insights into the truths of God's Word that you can pass along to your students or group members.

DESIGNED FOR QUICK ACCESS

Those with time constraints will especially appreciate the time-saving features built in the *Shepherd's Notes*. All features are intended to aid a quick and concise encounter with the heart of the message of this important book.

Concise Commentary. This feature enables the reader to grasp quickly the essentials of these three letters of John.

Outlined Text. A comprehensive outline, presented in the Table of Contents, covers the entire text of 1,2,3 John. This is a valuable feature for following the narrative's flow, allowing for a quick, easy way to locate a particular passage.

Shepherd's Notes. These summary statements appear at the close of every key section of the narrative. While functioning in part as a quick summary, they also deliver the essence of the message presented in the sections they cover.

Icons. Various icons in the margin highlight recurring themes in 1,2,3 John, aiding in selective searching or tracing of those themes.

Sidebars and Charts. These specially selected features provide additional background information to your study or preparation. These include definitions as well as cultural, historical, and biblical insights.

Maps. These are placed at appropriate places in the book to aid your understanding and study of a text or passage.

Questions to Guide Your Study. These thought-provoking questions and discussion starters are designed to encourage interaction with the truth and principles of God's Word.

In addition to the above features, study aids have been included at the back of the book for those readers who require or desire more information and resources for working through 1,2,3 John. These include a list of reference sources used for this volume, which offer many works that allow the reader to extend the scope of his or her study of 1,2,3 John.

DESIGNED TO WORK FOR YOU

Personal Study. Using the *Shepherd's Notes* with a passage of Scripture can enlighten your study and take it to a new level. At your fingertips is information that would require searching several volumes to find. In addition, many points of application occur throughout the volume, contributing to personal growth.

Teaching. Outlines frame the text of 1,2,3 John and provide a logical presentation of the message. *Shepherd's Notes* provide summary statements for presenting the essence of key points and events. Personal Application icons point out personal application of the message of 1,2,3 John, and Historical Context icons indicate where background information is supplied.

Group Study. Shepherd's Notes can be an excellent companion volume to use for gaining a quick but accurate understanding of 1,2,3 John. Each group member can benefit by having his or her own copy. The *Note's* format accommodates the study of, or the tracing of, the themes throughout 1,2,3 John. Leaders may use its flexible features to prepare for group sessions, or use during group sessions. Questions to Guide Your Study can spark discussion of the key points and truths of 1,2,3 John.

LIST OF MARGIN ICONS USED IN 1,2,3 JOHN

 Shepherd's Notes. Placed at the end of each section, a capsule statement provides the reader with the essence of the message of that section.

 Old Testament Reference. To indicate a prophecy fulfillment and its discussion in the text.

 New Testament Reference. Used when the writer refers to New Testament passages that are related to or have a bearing on the passage's understanding or interpretation.

 Historical Background. Historical Context. To indicate historical information—historical, biographical, cultural—and provide insight on the understanding or interpretation of a passage.

 Personal Application. Used when the text provides a personal or universal application of truth.

 Word Picture. Indicates that the meaning of a specific word or phrase is illustrated so as to shed light on it.

INTRODUCTION TO 1 JOHN

This letter is important and practical for the modern reader. It is a passionate letter written from a pastor to his flock. It is a letter written to the early church. It addresses a first-century situation. However, its message resonates with significant application for the church and the world today. The study of 1 John will assist believers in finding security, increasing joy, and moving forward in their faith while it also will serve as a reliable and poignant warning for the unbelievers.

Reading 1 John casually, one is struck by its simplicity. Reading and rereading it, one comes to discover its depth and complexity and to derive even greater benefit from it. First John is one book of the Bible that can assist even the simplest of readers, yet prompt the most skilled of scholars to scratch their heads while remaining uncertain as to the complete depth of the meaning within the text.

This letter is listed among the "General Epistles," but it is uniquely different from others included in this category. The message of 1 John and the means in which that message is communicated provide for exciting and rewarding study. In order to appreciate the details of the text itself, it will help to discuss a few introductory matters first.

The terms *General* or *Catholic* Epistles are traditional ways of designating the New Testament letters not attributed to Paul and written to a more general or unidentifiable audience: James; 1 and 2 Peter; 1, 2, and 3 John; Jude. The two shorter letters of John are included with 1 John even though they are seemingly addressed to specific readers.

AUTHORSHIP OF 1 JOHN

There is no signature on this letter. There are no obviously intentional clues given as to whom the author was. Traditionally, the apostle John, the son of Zebedee, the author of the Gospel known by his name, is credited with the authorship of

External/Internal Evidence

External evidence is information gained from a source outside the given text (here, 1 John). *Internal evidence* is information gained from the study of the given text.

The *Didache* is an early church manual of instruction regarding Christian life and church government that was composed no later than the early second century. Its longer title helps explain its nature: "The Teaching of the Lord, through the Twelve Apostles, to the Gentiles." The Muratorian Canon are those New Testament books recognized as Scripture by the church at Rome around A.D. 200. This list was first printed in 1740 by L. A. Muratori from an eighth-century manuscript.

this letter. There is both internal and external evidence that support this view, though there are admittedly some students who disagree with the traditional view.

The external evidence supports the conclusion that the apostle John wrote this letter. Allusions and veiled references to John's letters are found in many early patristic writings such as *Clement of Rome* and in the *Didache*, although they do not identify John as the author. Irenaeus (ca. A.D. 130–200) is noted as the first to clearly attribute 1 and 2 John to John, the apostle and author of the Fourth Gospel (*Against Heresies* 3.16.8). The Muratorian Canon testifies to the authority of John's letters and to John as the author. Origen (d. ca. A.D. 255) relied on 1 John, often naming John the apostle as its author. He was the first to include all three epistles as a part of John's work.

The internal evidence also points to John as the author. It does so in two ways. First, the internal evidence supports the conclusion that the author of the letter is the same as the author of the Fourth Gospel. If the author of that Gospel is John (as I believe him to be), there is good reason to believe he is also the writer of this letter. The discussion of authorship of the Gospel is much too complicated to be discussed in this book. For a concise argument for Johannine authorship of the Gospel, see Thomas D. Lea's book, *The New Testament*, pp. 153–256.

The Gospel of John and 1 John are clearly similar in both substance and syntax, providing further internal evidence for their having the same author. The author of each uses the same set of opposite phrases: "light and darkness," "life and death," "love and hate," and "truth and falsehood." People are placed in only one of two groups: "children of God" or "children of the devil"; they belong to the world or do not belong to the world; they have life and know God or they do not have life and do not know God. Both books use a similar Greek syntax involving the simplest of constructions filled with parallelisms. The Gospel and the letter have similar vocabulary and an overwhelmingly identical phraseology of ideas, such as believers being called God's "children," the Holy Spirit being the "Spirit of Truth," and the "remaining/abiding" union of believer and Christ, as well as many others. Therefore, there appears to be one author for both works. With this conclusion, whatever can be learned about the author of the Fourth Gospel can be said of the author of 1 John and vice versa.

The second way the internal evidence points toward John as the author is that the author claims to be an eyewitness to Jesus' life. In 1 John 1–4, he describes himself as one having had a close personal relationship with Christ. Throughout his letter he also writes as one having authority. His use of an authoritative tone (i.e., "my dear children," 2:1) and his authoritative commands all reveal his authoritative position. His authority and eyewitness testimony lead to the conclusion that the author of 1 John was an apostle.

Therefore, although he did not identify himself by name, the combination of all of these elements suggests that it is best to accept the apostle John, the son of Zebedee, the "disciple whom Jesus loved," as the author of 1 John.

The author of the Gospel of John refers to himself as the "disciple whom Jesus loved." In this way John revealed his personal and close relationship to Jesus and his presence with Him at some important moments. You can see John's relationship with Jesus as the "disciple whom Jesus loved" at the prediction of Judas's betrayal (John 13:23), when Jesus asked him from the cross to care for His mother (John 19:26–27), where John outran Peter to the empty tomb (John 20:2), when he followed the resurrected Jesus and Peter along the beach and became the subject of Peter's misdirected question (John 21:20), and when he identified himself as the one who wrote the Gospel (John 21:24).

The apostles were eyewitnesses who were also invested with authority from Jesus. "He appointed twelve—designating them apostles—that they might be with him and that he might send them out to preach and to have authority to drive out demons" (Mark 3:14–15).

Here is a snapshot of the author: Name: John. Nickname: Son of Thunder. Father: Zebedee. Mother: Salome, possibly a sister of Jesus' mother Mary. Brother: James. Hometown: Capernaum or Bethsaida in Galilee. Mid-life residence: Jerusalem. Later life residence: Ephesus. Family business: Fishing. Family class: Well-to-do enough to have servants. Political connections: Known by the high priest with access to his court. Calling: Apostle of Jesus. Closest ministry partners: James, his brother, and Simon Peter. Biblical writings: Gospel of John; 1, 2, 3 John; Revelation.

Elements of a Letter

Letters of this period had the following six elements: (1) the sender's name, (2) the recipient's name, (3) a greeting, (4) a prayer wish and/or thanksgiving, (5) the body of the letter, and (6) a final greeting and farewell.

LITERARY FORM OF 1 JOHN

First John is a letter that on the surface does not look like one. Interestingly, 1 John has none of the formal elements most letters of the period had except the body. Yet it was clearly a written document, not a sermon or homily (2:1, 12–14). Furthermore, it was written to a specific group of people with whom John had a relationship (see 2:7, 12–14, 19, 26). It appears to be a letter with the introductory and concluding elements cut off. Therefore, although it may read more like a homily or a theological treatise, it should be interpreted as a letter to a specific group of people for a specific occasion in a specific context.

RECIPIENTS AND ORIGINATION OF 1 JOHN

John does not directly tell who the recipients of his letter were, although it does appear that he had a specific audience in mind. This omission could be because he hoped it would be sent around to various churches in the area beyond the one specific church to whom he was writing. The designations "my dear children" (2:1) and "dear friends" (2:7) reveal his relationship with the recipients and his intention of sending it to these specific people. His knowledge of the situation and challenges facing the recipients (2:19; 5:13–14, 21) further support an intended audience. Even a superficial reading of the letter reveals the intimate care John had for the readers and the personal relationship they had together, even though he does not mention a single name.

Early church tradition claims that John spent the last part of his life living in and ministering around the city of Ephesus. Following the death of Mary, the mother of Jesus, tradition has it that

John moved to this area in the middle of the first century. Although it cannot be determined for certain, it appears that John wrote from Ephesus and sent his letter to the churches he had been ministering to in and around the city of Ephesus located in the Roman province of Asia.

DATE OF THE WRITING OF 1 JOHN

When did John write this letter? That is not an easy question. Evidence within the letter is very slight. The dating of the letter is generally tied to two issues: (1) the relationship of the date for 1 John as compared to that of the Gospel, and (2) the understanding of what type of false teaching John was writing to combat.

First John appears to have been written after the composition of the Gospel of John (A.D. 80–90). The Gospel was written for the purpose of evangelism (John 20:31) and the letter for the purpose of strengthening the faith of the believer (1 John 5:13). The letter appears to be answering follow-up questions generated from the Gospel and the misuse of the Gospel by the false teachers.

The letter seems to be combating a false teaching found in the latter part of the first century. John is concerned to strengthen his readers against the false claims of the Gnostic or proto-Gnostic teachers. This late first-century movement helps place John's letter in that time period.

Furthermore, John treated his readers as younger and of a different generation than he. All of this evidence supports a date later than the same author's Gospel and perhaps closer to the end of his life. Although it is difficult to date the letter precisely, it seems best to place it in the final decades if not the final decade of the first century (A.D. 85–95).

Some scholars distinguish between a "letter" and an "epistle." A letter is thought to be more personal and not written for public reading. An epistle was more of an artistic literary form intended to be read to the public. In this sense, 1 John would more formally be called an epistle while 2 and 3 John would be letters.

Ephesus was one of the largest and most impressive cities in the ancient world. It was a political, religious, and commercial center in Asia Minor with a population of more than 250,000 people, making it the fourth largest city in the world during the end of the first century. Paul, Timothy, and John all played a significant role in the spread of Christianity in and around Ephesus. The grandeur of the city was created by the temple of Artemis, the civic agora, the temple of Domitian, gymnasiums, public baths, a 24,000-seat theater, a library, public streets, a commercial agora, and many private homes.

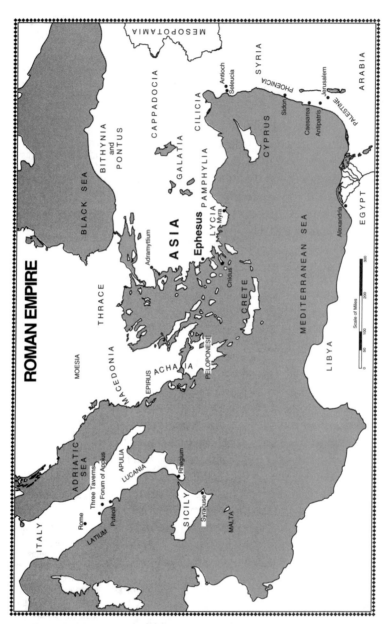

"The Roman Empire" from *Romans,* vol. 27, New American Commentary
(Nashville, Tenn. Broadman & Holman Publishers), 20.

THE PURPOSES OF 1 JOHN

Prior to delving into the text of any letter, it is helpful to know the purpose for which it was written. John's first letter has several specific and stated purposes. His purposes cover two general categories: pastoral and polemical.

John's pastoral purposes reveal his care for his flock and identify ways he desires them to be established in the Christian life. He listed four pastoral purposes: (1) to increase their fellowship with him (1:3); (2) to complete his and their joy (1:4); (3) to help keep them from sinning (2:1); and (4) to provide a foundation for the assurance of their salvation (5:13).

His polemical purpose reveals his understanding of the false teaching they were encountering and his desire to protect them from it (2:26; 3:7; 4:1–3). This polemical purpose is seen in nearly every verse of his letter as he fights both the theological and ethical errors of the false teachers invading the area around Ephesus. It is his pastoral care that drives his theological battle.

John also included a clearly stated purpose in his Gospel. He writes, "Jesus did many other miraculous signs in the presence of his disciples, which are not recorded in this book. But these are written that you may believe that Jesus is the Christ, the Son of God, and that by believing you may have life in his name" (John 20:30–31).

THE HERESY CONTESTED IN 1 JOHN

Since John's first letter is so driven by the false teaching from which he was trying to protect his flock, it is important for the student of this letter to gain a grasp of what the heretical teaching entailed. It is generally agreed that John directed much of his letter against a variety of Gnostic teachings. Gnosticism was one of the most dangerous heresies of the first two centuries of the church. It was a combination of oriental mysticism and Greek philosophy. It blended in just enough of the Christian perspective to make it an effective counterfeit Christianity. The Gnosticism in the first century was an early form of the more intricately developed system found in the second and third centuries.

Although the many Gnostic sects had variations in their systems, Gnosticism had two basic beliefs. First, knowledge was the one condition for salvation and the one test of fellowship with God. Faith was inferior to knowledge, and salvation was attained through enlightenment. The knowledge, however, that brought both faith in and fellowship with God was not an intellectual achievement, but it was a secret knowledge gained as a gift of revelation by God. What the precise knowledge was is quite vague, but it was considered different from and superior to the revelation found in the Scriptures. This belief led to a two-class division of Christians: the "haves" and the "have nots." Those with knowledge were considered the spiritual ones, and those without were called the carnal ones. This distorted emphasis led to arrogance, a lack of love, and exclusivism.

The second basic belief in Gnosticism was that all matter is inherently evil. This belief led Gnostics into numerous theological and ethical errors that ran head-on into the teachings of Christianity. Theologically, their most significant error was the denial of the real incarnation of God in Jesus. Since the body was evil, they believed the perfect God could not be united with it.

There were two different forms of Gnostic teaching concerning the denial of the incarnation. Docetic Gnosticism denied that Jesus was ever really human, but insisted He only seemed to be human. Jesus' body was only an illusion. Cerinthian Gnosticism (named after its teacher, Cerinthus) distinguished between the man Jesus and the divine Christ. Cerinthus claimed that Jesus

Gnosticism: The modern designation for certain religious and philosophical perspectives that existed prior to the establishment of Christianity and for the specific systems of belief, characterized by these ideas, which emerged in the second century and later. The term *gnosticism* is derived from the Greek word *gnosis* (knowledge) because secret knowledge was so crucial a doctrine in gnosticism (Harold S. Songer, "Gnosticism," *Holman Bible Dictionary*).

was a mere man who had the Spirit of Christ come upon Him at His baptism and leave Him just before His suffering on the cross. In this way, the divine Christ was not born nor did He suffer. He only came upon the man Jesus for a season. Both of these forms of Gnosticism can be detected in John's first letter as he counters them by teaching about the reality of the incarnation (4:1–3) and the unity of Jesus as the Christ from the beginning to the end of his life (5:6).

Ethically, the Gnostics' most significant error came as a result of their belief that matter was evil. This led them to two extremes. First, some Gnostics treated their bodies harshly (seen in the background of Colossians, especially 2:21–23). Second, some Gnostics treated their bodies and moral behavior with great licentiousness. Since the body and the spirit were separate, they believed it didn't matter what they did with their bodies. They set themselves above morality and agreed that nothing they did was sin. This second ethical extreme was the teaching that John was battling, leading to his insistence upon obedience to God.

This overview of the various teachings of Gnosticism should provide the reader of 1 John with a jump-start into discovering why John was written about certain issues and how the readers would have perceived his teachings. He most certainly was directing much of his letter against these Gnostic teachings that were finding their way into the churches. He wanted to protect his flock and clarify Christian doctrine.

THE STRUCTURE OF 1 JOHN

Setting forth the structure of 1 John has proven difficult since the time the letter was written. Some ancient interpreters saw no form at all to

"Docetic" comes from the Greek word *doke* which means "to seem."

Eusebius recorded the story of how the apostle John once scurried out of a public bath house when he learned that Cerinthus had come inside. While running away, he beckoned others to join him by yelling, "Let us flee, lest the bath fall; for Cerinthus, the enemy of the truth, is within." See Eusebius, *Church History*, 3.28.6.

this letter and thought of the writer as simply presenting his informal disconnected thoughts. A superficial reading of the text can reinforce this initial impression. Many today still hold to this view, seeing the sections of the letter to be connected by association of ideas rather than a logical flow of thought. Other commentators have interpreted the letter to have an exceptionally high degree of structure, while still others view the letter as having some structure. Since there does appear to be some logical structure, an understanding of the general framework of the letter should aid in proper interpretation.

This letter was written to people whose convictions and security were under attack. It was written to help provide assurance of who Christ is and of who really belongs to Christ. In order to bring about this assurance, John provided and repeated three tests by which a person can judge if he or she truly possesses eternal life. The three tests are moral, social, and theological, and they test a person's behavior, love, and beliefs, respectively. The repetitions of these three tests provide the skeletal structure of 1 John.

THE PRACTICAL VALUE OF 1 JOHN

As you engage in the study of this letter, you should not expect to find only an ancient message for those in the first century who were battling the burdens of Gnosticism. You can be assured that you will find a message for today that is powerful and applicable.

God has left for today's Christian a deposit of guidance and hope in this letter of John. There is guidance into the right way to live the Christian life and the right beliefs that are the basis of that life. There is hope in the assurance that can

Before you begin the study of this letter, it may be helpful to pause and consider modern teachings or ideas that are similar to Gnosticism. First John will help you counter those teachings from a Christian perspective and ground you in the correct doctrine that will sensitize you to counterfeits of Christian faith.

be gained through understanding the beliefs which are necessary for a person to receive eternal life and what characteristics that life will naturally produce. In an uncertain world, this book provides certainty. This benefit alone makes 1 John valuable for today.

- *First John is a letter written by the apostle*
- *John at the end of the first century to Christians in the area of Ephesus. John's desire*
- *was to gird them up in their faith so they*
- *would find assurance in their salvation and*
- *be equipped to refute the false teachers of the*
- *Gnostic movement. He did this in his letter*
- *with the repetition of three tests of life:*
- *moral, social, and doctrinal.*

QUESTIONS TO GUIDE YOUR STUDY

1. Who do you think wrote 1 John? What evidence can you give to prove your opinion?
2. What type of false teaching is encountered today that would be similar to Gnosticism?
3. What is the likely place and time when 1 John was written?

PREFACE: THE BASIS OF FELLOWSHIP AND JOY (1:1–4)

The first four verses of John's letter are unlike the beginning of most letters in the New Testament. There are no preliminaries. John quickly jumps to his point. The absence of such

This preface has many similarities to the prologue of John's Gospel (John 1:1–18). He used similar words in each (e.g., "word," "life," "witness") and parallel phrases (e.g., "In the beginning was the Word," and "That which was from the beginning"). Furthermore, both focus on the person of Jesus. The prologue, however, dwells upon His deity where the letter's preface turns the focus on His real humanity while acknowledging His deity. As in the Gospel, the initial verses of this letter dive headlong into the essential topics to be elaborated in the rest of the letter. After one paragraph, John challenged the false teaching and began to help his flock find security.

"In the beginning was the Word, and the Word was with God, and the Word was God. He was with God in the beginning . . . The Word became flesh and made his dwelling among us. We have seen his glory, the glory of the One and Only, who came from the Father, full of grace and truth" (John 1:1, 14).

expected elements draws attention to the urgency of the situation and leads the reader right into the heart of the letter. Although John did not use the traditional opening, he prefaced his letter with four verses of foundational matters concerning the apostolic proclamation (vv. 1, 3a), the source of the proclamation (v. 2), and its purposes (vv. 3b–4).

THE PROCLAMATION (1:1, 3A)

John began his letter by proclaiming to his readers what the apostles ("we proclaim") had proclaimed, namely, "the Word of life." But what is "the Word of life"? Since it is the subject of the proclamation, it becomes an important question. There are two possibilities. The first takes the phrase to be impersonal and means the life-giving message. The second possibility takes the phrase "the Word of life" to be personal and means the living Word of God. In this sense, it is a personal name for Jesus Christ. The earliest Greek manuscripts we have today are written with all capital letters (uncials) and provide no help in determining if the author wanted "Word" (*logos*) capitalized or not. The best support for this view comes from John's similar uses of the term *logos* in the prologue to his Gospel (John 1:1, 14) and in Revelation (19:13).

If John wrote his letters shortly after the Gospel and as a companion piece, then it seems he would be using the terms in the same way. Therefore, the second interpretation seems correct. The "Word of life" is Jesus Christ Himself. "Word" is a special, almost technical term that John borrowed from either Jewish or Greek use and redefined it to represent Jesus. Christ is the subject of the proclamation.

The substance of this proclamation is filled out with four relative clauses. These apparently were placed at the beginning of the sentence and the letter for emphasis. The first deals with Christ's eternal preexistence, and the last three deal with His humanity. Each serves both to strengthen the readers' understanding of who Jesus is and to confront the false teaching that challenged these understandings.

Why would John use the term *Word* (*logos*) for Jesus? The term *logos* was used in many different religious and philosophical contexts in the first century, and scholars suggest each of these as possible backgrounds for John's use. Whatever the background of the original readers, they would have had a familiarity with the term *logos* that we do not have today.

Jesus' eternal preexistence is confirmed in the first clause of the letter. "From the beginning" is equivalent to "from eternity." The phrase is used of the eternal God in 1 John 2:13–14 and of the sinning activity of Satan in 1 John 3:8. Although it is not stated with the exact same words as in the Gospel, the meaning appears to be the same. The Gospel claims that "in the beginning was the Word, and the Word was with God" (John 1:1). The letter claims "that which was from the beginning," and he "was with the Father" (1 John 1:3a). In every instance the verb ("was") is an imperfect tense, suggesting a continual existence that always has been. John's claim is that Jesus is preexistent, or, that he has always been.

An understanding of John's use of the various tenses of Greek verbs is critical for understanding some of his key points. The key to the tense is not so much the time of the action, but the type of action. Generally speaking, an "imperfect tense," a "present tense," and a "future tense" verb relate action that is ongoing in past, present, and future time, respectively. An "aorist tense" verb relates action that happened in the past with no type of results inferred. A "perfect tense" verb relates an action that occurred in the past, the effects of which remain in the present.

Moreover, John claimed that Jesus was really human. He succinctly unites the divine with the human, the timeless with the historical, the preexistent Word with the visible and tangible Jesus. By tying the doctrine he is about to teach to the authority that he had to teach it, John testified to his eyewitness account of the reality of Jesus' humanity.

The phrases "we have heard," and "we have seen with our own eyes" begin to prove the humanity of Jesus. Although Jesus existed from the beginning, John had heard Him and seen Him. Both statements are in the perfect tense, which

The Bible begins with the claim, "In the beginning God created the heavens and the earth" (Gen. 1:1). The first verse of the Bible assumes the existence of God and makes a reference to His activity at the beginning of time. John, in the Gospel and in this letter, indicated that when the beginning started, Jesus already was.

The Greek root word for "we have touched" (*pselaphao*) is a picturesque word. It means "to grope after," "to handle," or "to feel for something like a blind man in the dark." In this context it means to examine something closely. This examination of John and the apostles is one of the bases for our faith.

denotes a past action with present implications. They point to the many audible and visual experiences of the apostles. John adds "with our own eyes" to emphasize that the experiences were actual.

When John stated "we have looked at and our hands have touched," he developed his case even more. The tense changes from perfect to the aorist. This may indicate a single act in the past. If so, it probably referred to a time when John and the other apostles had seen and touched Jesus' resurrected body. John talked about such a time in his Gospel (John 20:24–29; cf. Luke 24:39). John emphasized his historical experience of seeing and touching Jesus, thereby testifying of His humanity.

■ *John began this preface with the subject of*
■ *his whole letter: Jesus Christ. Calling Him*
■ *"the Word of life," John proclaimed His deity*
■ *and His humanity and gave his eyewitness*
■ *account to support such claims.*

THE SOURCE OF THE PROCLAMATION (1:2)

Verse 2 serves as an aside or as a parenthesis in thought. John stopped in mid-sentence and explained how that which was from the beginning could have been experienced by the three main human senses. He did this by explaining that the life "appeared," before he elaborated on what the "life" in the "Word of life" is.

How was it possible for people to see, hear, and handle the eternal Word? John explained this in verse 2. Although "life" may be a reference to the life offered in Christ, it seems to be another distinct reference to Jesus Himself. This life is both "eternal"—a reference to a quality of life that transcends time—and "was with the Father," implying a face-to-face relationship.

John maintained that this "life appeared." The word "appear" can be translated "to manifest," "to reveal," and more literally means "to bring to light that which already exists." The life was manifested in a human body. John's testimony reveals the progressive experience of the human senses from the most unreliable to the most reliable, from the most abstract to the most tangible. He heard, saw, and felt the human body of Christ, proving it was real.

After the first sentence (vv. 1–3a), John took aim at the two primary tenets of the false teachers. To those who were claiming that Christ simply appeared to be human, John said he had heard, seen, and felt Him. To those who said the man Jesus was not the Christ, John said He was the one who was from the beginning. While declaring the foundation of his doctrine, John shot down the foundation of his opponents.

Jesus is referred to as "life" in other places by John. "And we are in him who is true—even in his Son Jesus Christ. He is the true God and eternal life" (1 John 5:20b). "In him was life, and that life was the light of men" (John 1:4). "Jesus answered, 'I am the way and the truth and the life'" (John 14:6).

What does faith in Jesus mean to you? If someone should ask you to explain why you believe in Jesus, could you give them a compelling reason? John helps us here. He gives an eyewitness testimony and passes it on to us so that our faith is more than "blind."

■ *John made such bold claims about who Jesus*
■ *is because Jesus appeared on the earth and the*
■ *apostles had physically encountered Him.*
■ *John's was a personal testimony of God in the*
■ *flesh.*

THE PURPOSES OF THE PROCLAMATION (1:3B–4)

With the two aspects of the apostolic proclamation out on the table (the preexistent [eternal] and human aspects of the Word of life), John gave the purposes of that proclamation in verses

"Fellowship" (*koinonia*) is a wonderful New Testament word. Its basic meaning is "to share something in common with another." Here it describes the unique Christian relationship that occurs when people share in common their experiences with Christ and their daily lives. True koinonia is a distinctly Christian experience.

Have you come to the place in your Christian walk where you understand that the Christian life is not a life lived in isolation? The New Testament writers, and especially John, would not recognize a "Lone Ranger" Christian. Fellowship is not only a luxury; it is a necessity in order for the Christian to grow to his or her fullest potential and to find true joy. Our twentieth-century culture pushes us away from honest, vulnerable relationships with others. What could you do today to increase your fellowship with other believers? Authentic church fellowship should always be in vogue.

3b and 4. John revealed two purposes for telling these readers about this apostolic proclamation.

The first purpose was for John's readers to have fellowship with him and with God (v. 3b). It is a natural result of the proclamation and acceptance of the Word of life. Salvation is understood to be the foundation for this fellowship, and fellowship is the visible social consequence of converted hearts. Community is created. The shared life is begun. Church happens when Christ is proclaimed and apprehended. Fellowship grows when life in Christ is the common thread and the central focus.

The second purpose is found in verse 4. John wanted their joy to be complete. He may echo the words of Jesus here as recorded in John's Gospel (15:11; 16:24). John reminded his readers of that teaching, clarifying that true joy is a result of true fellowship, which is a result of understanding and personally accepting the truth about Christ. In the churches that were about to be torn asunder by false doctrine, John gave a clarion call, proclaiming that the right doctrine doesn't pull people apart; it brings believers together.

In this preface, John took his readers from one extreme of eternity to the other while grounding them in the basics of true fellowship and true joy. With his final words being "make our joy complete," he described a perfect and permanent situation that will occur only in heaven (the Greek uses a perfect tense for "make complete"). In this way, he led his readers back to before time existed ("from the beginning," v. 1) and forward to when time as we know it will no longer exist. In order for them to experience this fellowship and joy, they must hold to the right

basis, which is the reality of the apostolic proclamation about Jesus Christ.

- *To a church under attack, John proclaimed*
- *who Jesus really is because he knew that an*
- *acceptance of this teaching would result in*
- *supernatural fellowship and joy. He intro-*
- *duced his letter with high expectations and*
- *solid confidence in their realization.*

QUESTIONS TO GUIDE YOUR STUDY

1. Why do you think John referred to Jesus
   as the "Word of life"?

2. If you were a Gnostic-type false teacher,
   what about this preface would bother
   you the most?

3. Write a clear, concise, and comprehensive statement about who Jesus Christ is
   and how you know that.

4. Does your church have authentic koinonia and joy? If so, what can you do to
   preserve it? If not, what steps can you
   take to help your church find it?

THE CHRISTIAN MESSAGE AND MORALITY (1:5–2:2)

Following the preface, John launched into a
description of who God is and the moral impli-
cation of His character on the character of true
believers. Verse 5 contains John's understanding of the basic Christian message. Based upon
that message, John then countered three different claims that the false teachers were making.

In John 15, Jesus
spoke about the
relationship of Himself
with the believer as a
vine is connected with
branches (an
important word picture
for "fellowship"). After
teaching with that
metaphor, he added,
"I have told you this so
that my joy may be in
you and that your joy
may be complete"
(John 15:11). Later,
Jesus stated, "Ask
and you will receive,
and your joy will be
complete" (John
16:24).

What John teaches is
that there is no real
fellowship resulting in
real joy outside of
Christ. This should
prompt us to
understand that all
meaningful
relationships will be
those in which each
person has been
initiated into saving
fellowship with Christ.
Are there
relationships that you
could naturally
deepen by introducing
your spouse, friend, or
family member to
Christ? Are there
relationships in which
you realize your level
of expected intimacy
is too high since
Christ is not a part of
them?

17

THE BASIC CHRISTIAN MESSAGE (1:5)

The apostle John had a basic but profound message about the character of God that he had "heard" and now was declaring. He could have heard this specific saying from Jesus, although it is nowhere recorded that Jesus made such a statement. Or, John could have meant that the substance of the revelation of God in the life of Christ was contained in this statement.

The statement of the message is simple and straightforward, but its meaning is evasive. The use of opposites and emphatic structures heighten the impact of the message. "Light" is placed first in the Greek sentence, highlighting its emphasis; while its opposite, "darkness," is used with a double-negative to underscore its emphasis.

John appears to attempt to define God in his writings. He said, "God is Spirit" (John 4:24); "God is love" (1 John 4:8); he "is true" (1 John 5:20); and "God is light" (1 John 1:5, cf. John 1:4). The writer of Hebrews added that God is a "consuming fire" (Heb. 12:29).

Some people think the statement "God is light" was a way of showing God's self-revealing character while others see it describing His moral purity. It probably means both. As it is natural for light to shine, so God is a revealing God. In opposition to the arrogant and elitist Gnostics who believed in a privately enlightened group, John declared, "God is light." He shines forth on everyone and is capable of being apprehended by all.

Light is not mixed with impurities. It is perfect, and cannot exist with darkness. As John wrote, "In him there is no darkness at all." If "light" is moral purity, then "darkness" is moral evil. God and sin are mutually exclusive.

- *All things are declared true or false based*
- *upon a standard. John preempted his discus-*
- *sion of the false claims with a presentation of*
- *a standard. The standard is God, and He is*
- *self-revealing and morally pure "light."*

CHRISTIAN MORALITY (1:6–2:2)

If God is light, then fellowship with Him is dependent on moral purity. False teachers were apparently teaching the opposite. To them, fellowship with God was not related to moral character.

In the next seven verses, the false claims can be read between the lines as John countered three false statements of this heresy. Each of John's statements follows a pattern.

(1) He introduced the false claim with an "if" statement and quickly refuted it in the same sentence.

(2) He altered the false claim to make it true in a second "if" statement.

(3) He gave the encouraging results that come when someone holds to that truth.

In this way John brought to light the false claims and went on to reveal a believer's true moral character. In each of the three teachings, John demonstrated how Christians must take sin seriously and how they must look to Christ for the solution to help sinners live in relationship with the light.

The First Claim and Its Refutation (1:6–7)

The first false assertion must have gone something like this: "It is possible to live in sin and

John used the pronoun "we" throughout this section. The use of "we" positioned John with his readers (not with the apostles as in the preface). In the first "if" statement of each new false claim, he used the "if we" to hypothesize what would happen if they adopted this false teaching. He then used "we" in the true statements to reveal universal principles applicable to all people—even the apostles.

The life of sin and the life for God are often referred to as "darkness" and "light," respectively, in the Bible. "The people walking in darkness have seen a great light; on those living in the land of the shadow of death a light has dawned" (Isa. 9:2).

"Everyone who does evil hates the light, and will not come into the light for fear that his deeds will be exposed" (John 3:20). "Then Jesus told them, 'You are going to have the light just a little while longer. Walk while you have the light, before darkness overtakes you. The man who walks in the dark does not know where he is going. Put your trust in the light while you have it, so that you may become sons of light'" (John 12:35–36a).

still have fellowship with God." But John said, "If we claim to have fellowship with him yet walk in the darkness, we lie and do not live by the truth" (v. 6). "Walk" is a present tense verb. The word commonly refers to a person's moral activity. In this tense it draws attention not to a few dark acts, but to the habitual lifestyle of walking in the darkness. John described a life lived in sin either void of adherence to God's self-revelation or filled with moral impurity.

The Gnostics believed that knowledge was the key to life and that righteous living was not important. To them, sin did not matter because righteousness and right moral conduct were of no value. Their claim was that an enlightened person could have fellowship with God and walk in sin at the same time.

John responded to this false claim boldly, declaring that the person "lies" and does not "live by the truth" (v. 6b). A person's words and his actions do not mesh with the truth. "Truth" relates to either right doctrine or correct conduct. Such a person speaks and lives a lie. Living in darkness makes fellowship with God impossible.

Gnosticism is not a formal religion today, but many people claim to have fellowship with the holy God even though they live a life of sin. John taught that religion without morality is an illusion. Can a person really be in the light while living a life in the darkness of sin? John said "no" to his first-century readers and he says the same to us today.

In verse 7 John showed what a true believer's lifestyle is like. It is to "walk in the light." Again, "walk" is in the present tense and reflects a habitual lifestyle of walking in the light of God's revelation in conformity with His moral standards.

Two benefits emerge from such a lifestyle (v. 7b). First, such people have fellowship "with one another." Who is "one another"? Some think this refers to Christians and God. Others think it refers to Christians and other believers. Each is possible, and each works hand in hand with the other. Since the life in darkness breaks fellowship, the life in the light naturally bonds fellowship. John included himself in the circle of fellowship by saying, "we have fellowship."

The second benefit arises naturally from the first: The believer is cleansed from all sin. "Blood" is a word in the New Testament that represents all that Christ did for us through His perfect life and sacrificial death. The blood of Christ does more than forgive; it erases the stain, "it purifies us from all sin." How this happens is not clear, but God said it does happen and for that we are deeply glad.

■ *An authentic Christian cannot live a lifestyle*
■ *of habitual sin. The Christian's life is one of*
■ *moral purity that produces fellowship with*
■ *God because of the purification from sin that*
■ *He gives us.*

The Second Claim and Its Refutation (1:8–9)

Verse 8 contains the second false claim. This one moves a step farther from the truth. To claim that you live in sin but that sin doesn't affect your fellowship with God is one thing. To claim that you have no sin is quite another.

The denial of these people must have been bold. "Sin" is again in the singular and more than likely refers to the principle of sin, or specifically, the sinful nature. The heretical teachers may have maintained that those who had been enlightened with their *gnosis* were also cured of their sinful natures. Or, they may have been claiming that though they sinned in their bodies, the flesh had nothing to do with their spirits.

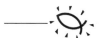

"In him we have redemption through his blood, the forgiveness of sins, in accordance with the riches of God's grace that he lavished on us with all wisdom and understanding" (Eph. 1:7–8). "To him who loves us and has freed us from our sins by his blood, and has made us to be a kingdom and priests to serve his God and Father—to him be glory and power for ever and ever! Amen!" (Rev. 1:5b–6).

It is important to notice how meticulous John chose his words. He highlighted exactly whose blood it is that does the work of purification. It is Jesus' blood. More specifically, Jesus is God's son ("Jesus, his son"). John probably chose these words carefully. He revealed that Christ was genuinely human and, therefore, qualified to offer the sacrifice for humanity. Also, he revealed that Jesus was God's Son and, therefore, able to be the perfect sacrifice.

John's readers who were especially familiar with the Old Testament would understand the importance of "blood." The Old Testament Jews regarded the blood of a person or animal as representing its physical life. To give up the blood was to give up the life.

To "confess our sins" means more than simply admitting them. The verb literally means "to speak the same thing," or "to agree with." It provides a word picture of confession as a nodding of the head in agreement with God's judgment on our act. We admit to God our guilt.

In either case, they were boldly declaring themselves to be without sin.

John quickly contradicted their teaching. "If we claim to be without sin," he declared, "we deceive ourselves." People who make this claim are out of touch with reality. Their lives are built on a shaky foundation.

The positive claim is given in verse 9. Confession, not denial, is the beginning answer to our sin problem. What is it that we are to confess? John declared, "our sins." This word is now plural ("sins"). John taught that confession is specific and particular, not general. It involves consciously calling to mind each sinful deed, one by one, admitting with God that it was wrong, and then forsaking the sin. Christians don't deny their sinful bent. They acknowledge it and then confess to God specific sins as they are brought to awareness.

The results of confession are both forgiveness and purification. Sins are forgiven because they are seen as debts that are released. The sinner is purified because sin is like a stain that needs to be removed.

God has promised to forgive sin upon our repentance. To this promise He is both faithful and just. It's clear what God's faithfulness means in this context. What does it mean to say God is just to forgive us our sins? It is not just for a holy God to allow sin to be removed and the sinner to be released. Justice implies that deeds receive what they deserve. Here is the marvel of grace. Jesus took the consequences of our sins. The nail scars on Christ portray the Father's justice. Forgiveness is "just" because Jesus shed His blood for the sinner. He received our punishment for us. God is "faithful" because He does what He promised and this because His Son died in our place.

- No matter what a person claims, an authentic
- Christian cannot deny his or her sinful nature.
- The Christian's life is one of regular and spe-
- cific confession that finds real forgiveness and
- purification from a faithful and just God.

The Third Claim and Its Refutation (1:10–2:2)

The third false claim is found in verse 10. It goes even one step deeper into heresy, and it is the most blatant denial of all. Whereas the first false claim was that a person could sin and still be in fellowship with God, and the second was that sin is not a part of one's personal nature, the third false claim dares to state that the enlightened have never sinned. To disagree that fellowship with God is broken by sin, or that sin is still a part of your nature is totally wrong, but to go on and claim that one has never sinned is to call God a liar. The climatic ascension of error is also seen in the corresponding counters offered by John: "we lie" (v. 6), "we deceive ourselves" (v. 8), and "we make him out to be a liar" (v. 10).

The false claim was that they had never committed an act of sin. "We have not sinned" translates a verb in the perfect tense. John used this to describe a person claiming to be in a condition of never having committed a sinful deed.

God has spoken. He has declared that all people have sinned. Moreover, God has provided a solution to our sinful condition. To deny what God has said—to deny what one is and has

John indicated it is the regular and specific listing of our sins before God that is the substance of true confession. How can we really be sorry and admit our mistakes if we can't detail them? How can we feel our need for forgiveness if we don't see our sin up close and personal?

Speaking of Jesus, Paul said, "whom God displayed publicly as a propitiation in His blood through faith. This was to demonstrate His righteousness, because in the forbearance of God He passed over the sins previously committed; for the demonstration, I say, of His righteousness at the present time, so that He would be just and the justifier of the one who has faith in Jesus" (Rom. 3:25–26, NASB).

"This is the covenant I will make with the house of Israel after that time,' declares the LORD. 'I will put my law in their minds and write it on their hearts. I will be their God, and they will be my people . . . . For I will forgive their wickedness and will remember their sins no more'" (Jer. 31:33–34b).

For the first time, John referred to his readers as "dear children." He did this eight other times in this letter (2:12, 13, 18, 28; 3:7, 18; 4:4; 5:21). The designation reveals John's older age, his authoritative position, and his tender care of the readers. This (2:2) is the only time he called them his children ("my"), portraying an especially tender touch.

been—is to put oneself beyond the solution God offers for sin.

John broke his parallel pattern in 2:1–2. He did not begin with an "if" clause; instead, he began with a direct statement, addressing his readers in an affectionate way.

John countered the false claim of verse 10 with two important and integrated thoughts. First, his purpose in writing this to them is so they will not sin. Second, if they do sin, he wanted them to know of God's plan for their sinfulness. Both ideas must be maintained; both thoughts must be balanced.

John declared that the reason why he is writing to them is so they will not commit a single act of sin. The tense of the verb (aorist) speaks of acts of sin, not a habitual lifestyle. John did not want them to be generally godly people. He desired for them to be people who "will not sin." This is the ideal.

John understood that this ideal will not often be met, so he quickly acknowledged that by saying, "But if anybody does sin." Again, the tense is aorist ("does sin") and reveals that John did believe that specific acts of sin are possible in a believer's life, although later he spoke in more detail about the incongruity of a sinful lifestyle with the believer.

If this sinless ideal is not met, John reminded his readers that God has made provision. The provision is found in Jesus Christ, who is presented in three roles. First, he is the "one who speaks to the Father in our defense." When a believer sins, Christ pleads his or her case to God. What is the case He pleads? It is not a plea of innocence or even a plea for mercy. Christ is the perfect advocate for the believer because His case is built on His applying His death to our misdeeds.

Second, Jesus is able to take care of our sin because he is "the Righteous One." The name *Jesus* highlights His humanity and, therefore, His understanding. The name *Christ* highlights His messianic office and, therefore, His qualification to help. The title "Righteous One" emphasizes His ability to approach God on our behalf. The Sinless One can approach the holy and plead the case of the sinful ones.

Third, Jesus is able to forgive our sinful acts because His is the "atoning sacrifice" for all sins. This "atoning sacrifice" is currently available. He "is" (present tense) still the "propitiation" for the believer and for the whole world. His death is not effective for the whole world; it is only available to the whole world. It must be accepted by faith to gain its benefit. John clearly stated this teaching in his writings (1 John 4:9, 14; John 1:29; 3:16; 5:24).

"One who speaks in our defense" translates one Greek word (*parakletos*). It is found in the New Testament only here and in the teachings of Jesus during His farewell discourse (John 14:16, 26; 15:26; 16:7). Jesus used it of the Holy Spirit and indirectly about Himself (calling the Holy Spirit "another" *parakletos*, John 14:16). John used it here as a reference to Jesus. The word literally means "one called alongside to help another," and it is often used of a counsel for the defense in a legal setting. The Holy Spirit as *parakletos* pleads Christ's causes against a hostile world; Christ pleads the believer's case against Satan (Rev. 12:10) and "to the Father."

■ *No matter what a person claims, all people*
■ *have committed acts of sin. The Christian*
■ *tries not to sin, but recognizes sin when it is*
■ *committed. A believer's hope is not for*
■ *strength not to sin, but it rests on Jesus*
■ *Christ, the Righteous One, the atoning sacri-*
■ *fice for our sins. All three false claims have*
■ *been refuted and the picture of a real Chris-*
■ *tian has been composed, revealing the right*
■ *attitude toward sin.*

QUESTIONS TO GUIDE YOUR STUDY

1. How would a first-century person living around Ephesus have understood John's

The main idea behind the word translated "atoning sacrifice" (*hilasmos*) is "to appease an offended person," and it is translated in the KJV as "the propitiation." John presented Jesus Christ not as the one who offers the appeasement, but as the offering itself. He is "the propitiation," "the atoning sacrifice" which appeased the wrath of God. God is just. Wrong must be paid for. But God Himself in the person of His Son takes the punishment for our sins.

statement: "God is light"? Would it be understood differently today?

2. What were the three false claims John refuted in this section of his letter?

3. How does the regular and specific confession of sins for forgiveness relate to the forgiveness that comes once and for all at salvation?

4. Are there any warnings that churches should be giving "nominal Christians" as a result of John's teachings in this section of his letter? Are there any different practices in which churches should be involved?

THE FIRST APPLICATION OF THE TESTS OF LIFE (2:3–27)

With the third verse of chapter two, we begin to study the third major section of John's first letter. In this section John presented the first round of his three tests by which the readers can judge if they possess eternal life. Between the lines of each test you can read the arguments of the false teachers which prompted John to discuss these issues. You can also see the solid application of the biblical doctrine of salvation that holds true for every generation.

The tests are moral, social, and doctrinal in nature, and they test, respectively, a person's behavior, beliefs, and attitude. While each test serves as a measure for assurance of salvation (or a prompt to the validity of the lack of it), each test also presents a challenge to the believer to become truer to the characteristic measured in the test.

THE MORAL TEST: A CALL TO OBEDIENT BEHAVIOR (2:3–6)

The structure of this paragraph is simple and somewhat repetitive. John began in verse three by stating the test. Verse 4 states the negative side of the same test. In verse 5 the test is elaborated, and in verse 6 it is made more specific with a call to action. The paragraph is an encouragement for assurance and an exhortation to action.

An Encouragement for Assurance (1 John 2:3–5a)

As the initial test is presented in verse 3, two foundational truths are also revealed. John indicated that we can both know Jesus and know that we know Him. In the face of a heresy which claimed that only certain special people were chosen to receive knowledge (*gnosis*), John declared we can know God and know that we do. He used the word "know" in two different ways: (1) We can know intellectually and experientially and (2) we can have intimate and saving fellowship with Jesus Christ.

The question now becomes, How can we know that we know Him? The answer to that question provides the substance of the first test of life. John made it clear, "We know that we have come to know him if we obey his commands" (2:3). The test is the test of behavior. In order to pass the test and gain assurance of salvation, a person must be obedient to God's commands. It is that simple. Obedient behavior is the sign of a life that is saved and in relationship with Jesus.

John reiterated this test in three different ways. In verse 3 he used the idea of obedience to God's "commands"—referring to the specific commands in Scripture or to Jesus' explicit

Twice in this section John used his common phrase "in this" (at the beginning of verse 3, not translated in the NIV; and in verse 5b "This is how"). Throughout this letter it is difficult to know if the phrase points forward or refers to what has already been said. In most cases, as in both of these occurrences, it appears to point forward to what is about to be said.

There are two Greek words translated by the English word *know* (*ginosk* and *oida*), but generally they are quite similar in meaning. One meaning is "intellectual knowledge" that is often gained by experience. It is the second meaning that John uses characteristically. This is the kind of knowledge that comes from intimate fellowship with God.

"Remain in me, and I will remain in you. No branch can bear fruit by itself; it must remain in the vine. Neither can you bear fruit unless you remain in me. I am the vine; you are the branches. If a man remains in me and I in him, he will bear much fruit; apart from me you can do nothing" (John 15:4–5). Each word translated "remain" in this passage is the same Greek word translated "to live" in 1 John 2:6.

commands. In verse 5 he stated it as obedience to God's "word"—referring to the total revelation of His will in the Scriptures. In verse 6 he described it as walking as Jesus walked—referring to the perfect portrayal of God's moral will in the life of Jesus. In each case, John used a present tense verb as a way of describing a lifestyle of obedience.

It doesn't matter if a person claims to know God; the test is found in the lifestyle one lives. If a person is an authentic Christian, he or she will have a lifestyle of obedience. If there is not a lifestyle of obedience, then the person claiming to know God is in reality "a liar, and the truth is not in him" (2:4).

While repeating the test, verse 5 also presents a result of obedience to God's Word. John wrote, "God's love is truly made complete in him." In obedience, love is "made complete"—not perfect, but brought to its proper end. True love is voiced best not in language, but in action.

An Exhortation for Action (1 John 2:5b–6)

The climactic description of the test comes in verse 6 as well as the natural call to action that should follow. John set up the test of verse 6 with his familiar "this is how we know" in verse 5b. While verse 3 talks about knowing God, and verse 5 refers to being "in him," verse 6 underscores the intimacy of the relationship by using the term "remaining/abiding" in him (NIV translates as "to live"). This word brings the test to a descriptive crescendo with an echo of John's earlier presentation of Jesus' vine and branches metaphor. It relates the continual aspect of the relationship between God and the person who truly knows Him.

The test is made even more specific. Obedience to God's "commands" or "word" is now illustrated with Jesus' life. An authentic Christian is one who walks as Jesus walked. "Walk" is a figurative word for how you conduct your life, how you live, what you do. To be in Him is to live like Him.

Not only does this become an illustration of the test; it also serves as an exhortation to action. "Must" is a business term that means we are "obligated" or "in debt" or "bound." The person who is in relationship with Jesus must not only follow His commands, but must act like Him as well. Our actions are not only a test of our relationship, but our Christlike actions are an obligation of our relationship.

In this brief clause, John simplified all the ethical commands and teachings of the Scriptures into a perfect picture of a person who exemplifies them all. A real Christian is one who is true to his or her name—a Christlike one. A truly authentic Christian must walk as Jesus walked.

- *The first and most obvious test to see if a per-*
- *son knows Christ is the test of obedient moral*
- *behavior. The encouragement for assurance*
- *and the exhortation for action are found in*
- *obeying God's commands, His Scripture, and*
- *walking like Jesus walked. These actions are*
- *the evidence for assurance of salvation.*

QUESTIONS TO GUIDE YOUR STUDY

1. Based upon this test, what counsel would you give to a person who doubts his or her salvation?

Upon reflection of Jesus' initial call found in Matt. 4:19, "Come, follow me" and his closing exhortation found in John 20:21, "As the Father has sent me, I am sending you," T. B. Maston wrote, "One test of whether we have heard and responded to His invitation, 'Come, follow me,' is whether we have heard and heeded His exhortation or command to go" (T. B. Maston, *To Walk as He Walked*, 1985, 27).

There are two things you should do after hearing John's exhortation for action. First, you should study the Gospels to learn about Jesus' life. To attempt to walk like Jesus walked without knowing how He walked will lead to further false teaching and living. John presupposed that these people had knowledge or factual information about what Jesus' life was like, probably because they had his Gospel. Second, you should commit to apply all that you learn about Jesus to your lifestyle.

2. What are some things that Jesus did that would *not* apply to our lives? What would apply?

THE SOCIAL TEST: A CALL TO A LOVING ATTITUDE (2:7–11)

After showing that moral obedience is a test of relationship with God, John then drew out one specific aspect of that obedience. Though specific, it may also be said that this new command envelops all the other commands. This is the social test—the test of love.

There were two basic words for "new" in the Greek of the New Testament. *Neos* signifies new in respect of time. It is used to say something is recent or young. *Kainos* signifies new in respect of quality or character. It is used to say something is different or novel. You may buy the most recent, brand new (*neos*) computer, but if you buy one that is revolutionary in its technology, it would be a new (*kainos*) type of computer. In both verse 7 and 8, John used *kainos* to signify that this command is not a novel one, but then again it is. When Jesus referred to the command to love as a "new" command in John 13:34, he also used the word *kainos*.

Once again, John did not deal with a hypothetical situation. He did not set up a straw man to knock down. He dealt with a real situation. If we are correct in our understanding of the background of this letter, the Gnostic teachers had created the need for this test. These people were arrogant, exclusive, and unloving. John called his readers to a test and to a lifestyle of love.

An Old-New Command (1 John 2:7–8)

John transitioned into his second test with a discussion of a command that is both old and new. He began in verse 7 with an affectionate term of address that is literally "beloved" ("dear friends," NIV); he used the same word in 3:2, 21; 4:1, 7, 11)—an appropriate address in light of the coming topic. What this command is, we are never clearly told, but it seems to be the command to love others that is discussed in verses 9–11.

John first declared that it is not "a new command but an old one" (v. 7a). By new (*keinen*) he meant novel, or new in kind or quality. It was not a novel idea; it was an "old" command. They should have been familiar with it because John said they have had it "since the beginning." John referred to the beginning of their experience as

Christians as he did in 2:24, 3:11, and 2 John 6 with this identical expression (the same phrase is also used of the beginning of Creation in 1 John 1:1 and John 1:1). The command to love has been around since Old Testament times (Lev. 19:18; Deut. 6:5). The point is that this teaching is not novel like the Gnostic's "new" teaching. It has been in effect for a long time, and they had heard it (v. 7b) through the teaching of Jesus presented in John's Gospel.

Verse 8 appears to be a contradiction, but it is not. It is a further teaching about this old-new command. John declared, "Though this is old, in another sense this command is radically a new kind of command." The command is to love one another as Jesus did. John went on and said "its truth," meaning the reality of its newness, "is seen in him and in you." The idea of love was not new, but Jesus filled the old command with new meaning. Its newness can be seen in several ways:

- In its authority: Jesus took the old command and put His sanction upon it (John 13:34).

- In its standard: Jesus filled the command with new meaning by presenting His own love as the model for ours (John 13:34). We are not to love others so much as we would love ourselves, but as Christ Himself loved us. This is an incredibly high standard.

- In its emphasis: Jesus tied all the teachings of the Law and the Prophets together with the command to love (Matt. 22:37–40). It is new in that its emphasis is central to obedience and is to be primary in our behavior.

The Old Testament clearly mandated love toward other people and God. "Do not seek revenge or bear a grudge against one of your people, but love your neighbor as yourself. I am the LORD" (Lev. 19:18). "Love the LORD your God with all your heart and with all your soul and with all your strength" (Deut. 6:5).

"Darkness" is a term that John uses with double meaning. Although it can mean "to be absent of physical light," its most prominent meaning is "the realm of spiritual decay, evil, and hopelessness." When Judas left the disciples to betray Jesus, John succinctly added, "And it was night" In this letter, John continued to use the physical picture of "darkness" to draw out the spiritual reality of the nonbeliever's world—a dark, evil world.

John used this word for "true" (*alethinos*) over twenty-three times in his writings, including four times in 1 John (it is used only five other times in the New Testament). He used it in several ways to describe Jesus. John said He is the "true light" (John 1:9; 1 John 2:8), the "true bread from heaven" (John 6:32), the "true vine" (John 15:1), and even the "true God" (1 John 5:20).

- In its extent: Jesus clearly taught that the love He was promoting was a love irrespective of race, social status, sex, or any other potential inhibitors. Everyone is our neighbor, and our love should extend to all our neighbors (Luke 10:25–37) and even to our enemies (Matt. 5:44).

- In its experience: As the truth of its newness is seen "in you" (1 John 2:8), the experience of the newness of the command is realized every moment a believer practices it. It creates a new way of life in us.

The reason the reality of the newness could be seen was "because the darkness is passing and the true light is already shining" (1 John 2:8c). The "darkness" is the present age of the world. In John it represents the arena of sin, ignorance, and absence from God. It is the old order. The "true light" is Jesus Himself. He is "true" not in the sense that a statement is true as opposed to false, but He is the genuine or real thing as opposed to unreal. We experience the reality of this new command because it is a part of the new age that is coming as the darkness passes away and the light continues to shine.

The Test of Love (1 John 2:9–11)

Having set the test up with the explanation of the command (vv. 7–8), John now moved directly into his second test of life. In the first test (vv. 3–6) he gave the principle followed by an example. Here he gave the example (v. 9) followed by the general principle (vv. 10–11). This is the moral test, and it calls the reader to investigate his or her loving attitude.

The false claim is revealed in verse 9. Anyone who claims to be in the light but lives a life of hate is making a false claim. The falsity of their claim is uncovered now, not by their disobedience, but by their hatred. The word "hates" in verses 9 and 11 relates a fixed and settled way of living (present tense). A person cannot simultaneously walk in hate and in the light. Darkness is the realm for hate. If a person lives a lifestyle of hatred, he or she fails the test and is "still in the darkness."

Next, John gave the general principle. It is first stated positively (vv. 10), then negatively (v. 11). A person either lives a life of hatred or love and finds himself either in the light or in the dark. There is no middle ground.

If a person "loves his brother," two things are true. First, he "lives in the light." The test is a lifestyle of love. If that is the lifestyle, John said that person "lives in the light"—the person is a true believer.

Second, if a person "loves his brother," then he has "nothing in him to make him stumble." That phrase can be translated "there is nothing to cause himself to stumble" or "there is nothing to cause others to stumble." Literally it says, "A stumbling block is not in him." Not only do those who love walk in the light, but they also have nothing to stumble over or anything to cause others to stumble.

The person who hates his brother experiences three negative effects (v. 11). First, he exists in the darkness ("is in the darkness"). In verse 9 John made the statement emphatic by saying he is in the darkness "until now" ("still," NIV). He is a person who has not experienced a life-changing relationship with the "true light," Jesus Christ. Second, he also "walks" in the darkness. He lives his life as a person in the darkness with no firm stance, no confident character, no ability to live like someone in the light. Finally, he

The word for *love* in this passage is a form of the Greek word *agape*. Many people are familiar with the various Greek words for *love*. There are three: *agapao* (and the noun *agape*), *phileo*, and *eros*. *Agape* carries the general meaning of "God's kind of love." It is a perfect, sacrificing, and caring love. *Phileo* means a tender affection and is often thought of as "friendship love" (seen in the name Philadelphia). *Eros* is a passionate type of love from which we get our word *erotic*. *Eros* is not used in the New Testament. Although the words *agape* and *phileo* often carry these unique meanings, at times they share a similar meaning. Here, however, in 1 John, the test of love is clearly a call to "God's kind of love" to be activated in the believer's life. It is more than an emotion (as it is popularly defined); it is about an attitude that prompts action.

If love is the key that keeps us from causing others to stumble, then love we must. The words of Jesus provide even more powerful motivation. "Jesus said to his disciples: 'Things that cause people to sin are bound to come, but woe to that person through whom they come. It would be better for him to be thrown into the sea with a millstone tied around his neck than for him to cause one of these little ones to sin. So watch yourselves'" (Luke 17:1–3a).

The command to love one another is repeated at least a dozen times in the New Testament. See John 13:34; 15:9, 12, 17; Rom. 13:8; 1 Thess. 4:9; 1 Peter 1:22; 1 John 3:11, 23; 4:7, 11, 12; 2 John 5. To see how practical love can be, take a concordance and look up the many "one another" passages in the New Testament.

has no direction: "He does not know where he is going."

John explained why this is so. He cannot find direction "because the darkness has blinded him." Hatred has distorted his perspective; it has stolen his ability to see. A. T. Robertson wrote about the blinding power of darkness: "In the Mammoth Cave of Kentucky the fish in Echo River have eyesockets, but no eyes" (A. T. Robertson, *Word Pictures in the New Testament*, vol. 6, 212). Furthermore, this may suggest that persons of hate cannot really see where they are headed. They are walking headlong into eternal moral and spiritual darkness.

■ *The command to love is as old as God's relat-*
■ *ing to His people and definitely familiar to*
■ *these believers because it was a part of the*
■ *original instructions which they received.*
■ *Yet, this old command has received new*
■ *meaning as "love" was fleshed out before us*
■ *in Jesus' life. Whether a person has this*
■ *"new" kind of love in his or her life is the test*
■ *of salvation.*

QUESTIONS TO GUIDE YOUR STUDY

1. How would you define the concept of love to a child?
2. In what ways did Jesus make new the old command to love?
3. Do you think it is possible to examine a person's attitude and action of love and determine if he or she is a believer? Why?

AN ASIDE ABOUT THE CHURCH
(2:12–14)

As you read through this letter, the paragraph that begins in verse 12 appears to be an intrusion into the thought of John. The address becomes more personal, the structure turns more poetic, and the content seems out of context. For these reasons some scholars argue that the text is not authentic or a later addition. However, this is an unnecessary conclusion.

Although the landscape of the text changes for a few verses, these words are an appropriate aside about the believers to whom John is writing. After giving some critical remarks and some decisive claims about what an authentic believer is, and preparing to make a few even more exacting and searching claims, John paused to assure his readers of what he believed to be true about their faith. He wanted to take away the false assurance of the heretical teachers, but he did not want to put undue doubt in the Christians. He wanted to assure the true believers.

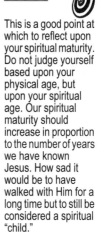

This is a good point at which to reflect upon your spiritual maturity. Do not judge yourself based upon your physical age, but upon your spiritual age. Our spiritual maturity should increase in proportion to the number of years we have known Jesus. How sad it would be to have walked with Him for a long time but to still be considered a spiritual "child."

In these three verses John used six statements, each revealing why he was writing: he knew of their authentic Christian faith. Each of the statements made that point in a slightly different way. The six statements break down into two sets of three statements (vv. 12–13b; 13b–14).

John used three different terms of address: "dear children," "fathers," and "young men." To whom do these terms refer? The best solution sees these three groups as representing three different levels of spiritual maturity: newborns in Christ (dear children), more developed believers (young men), and strong and mature Christians (fathers).

John used two different words for "dear children." In verse 12 he called them *teknia*, and in verse 13c he called them *paidia*. Generally, *teknia* carries the idea of relationship or affection (and so, "dear children"), and *paidia* relates the idea of inferiority or age subordination (and so, "little children"). John probably used the words interchangeably without any distinction in meaning since he used both to refer to all the believers together in 2:1 (*teknia*) and 2:18 (*paidia*).

The psalmist had the same type of understanding about God as these "fathers." "Lord, you have been our dwelling place throughout all generations. Before the mountains were born or you brought forth the earth and the world, from everlasting to everlasting you are God" (Ps. 90:1–2). Malachi revealed God declaring about Himself, His consistent character: "I the LORD do not change" (Mal. 3:6).

John wrote to each group for a different reason and one that was appropriate for their spiritual maturity level. In all six statements the verb used to describe that maturity level is a perfect tense. It relates the present consequence of a past action.

The children have assurance because their "sins have been forgiven" (v. 12). This is the beginning of the Christian life and is the foundation for new life. The perfect aspect means their sins were forgiven in the past (when they put their faith in Christ), and the results still remain. The phrase "on account of his name" means their faith was based upon Jesus' revealed character. A person's "name" represented his or her character. Forgiveness is based upon who Christ is and what He has done.

The second address to the "dear children" (v. 13c) highlights the same idea of forgiveness as in the first. "Having known the Father" means to be in relationship with Him, which is only accomplished through forgiveness. Also, John's use of the word "Father" points out who Christ is again. As in verse 12, He is God's Son.

The "fathers" have assurance because they "have known him who is from the beginning" (identical in verses 13a and 14a). The same verb ("have known") is used here as with the "children" in verse 13c. It signifies not head knowledge as much as relational experience. The emphasis for the "fathers" is, however, in the degree of knowledge. "Him" may refer to God or to Jesus. John left it vague. All believers know God and Jesus, even spiritual babes or "children," but mature believers know Him in a deeper sense. If "Him" refers to God, the "fathers" know Him as the one who "is from the beginning," the one who is consistent and never changing. If "Him" refers to Jesus, the "fathers" know Him as the preexistent Christ (as in 1 John 1:1).

The "young men" have assurance because they are victorious over evil. They "have overcome the evil one" (vv. 13b, 14c). Those people who are not new to their faith and who have not grown old with their beliefs are the very people who are engaged in the battle of Christian living. Theirs is not so much a fresh experience with forgiveness or a peaceful touch of fellowship as it is a war with the enemy. So, John encouraged these "adolescent" Christians by reminding them that they have already overcome and remain victorious (the perfect tense again). The victory may have been over the heretical teachers or it may have been over a variety of evils.

Two further qualities of these "young men" are mentioned in verse 14. First, they "are strong." This strength surely has more to do with spiritual might that physical fortitude. Second, they are intimately tied to the Word of God: "the word of God lives in you." The "word" here is the same as is used for Jesus (*logos*), but here it means the gospel message. They have made the truth behind that message and its ethical teachings a part of their lives. Both of these statements use present tense verbs, demonstrating that these are permanent and dynamic forces in their lives.

- *John stopped for a moment to give his readers*
- *assurance. Based upon his relationship with*
- *them, he encouraged each person according*
- *to his or her own level of maturity. A person*
- *can find assurance at whatever stage of*
- *Christian maturity they have achieved.*

"How can a young man keep his way pure? By living according to your word" (Ps. 119:9).

Jesus gave assurance to believers in the same way as John did here with the young men. "To the Jews who had believed him, Jesus said, 'If you hold to my teaching, you are really my disciples'" (John 8:31). "Hold" translates the same verb as in 1 John 2:14. Again, the same word is used by Jesus but it is translated "remain" in John 15:7: "If you remain in me and my words remain in you, ask whatever you wish, and it will be given you."

By describing the assurance of these "young men" who are in the process of growth, John gave three steps to Christian growth: Be strong, by being studious, so you can be striving for real growth and effective Christian living. We have no chance of growing into maturity outside of the study of God's Word.

AN ASIDE ABOUT THE WORLD (2:15–17)

The topic now changes and so does the mood. The theme is not assurance, but warning. The tense is not the perfect, but the present imperative—the mood of command. In the midst of assurance, the believers needed to be aware of the reality of temptation. So John commanded them, "Do not love the world or anything in the world" (1 John 2:15a). That is the central thought of this aside about the world. The rest of the paragraph gives support to this command by explaining two reasons why it should be heeded.

The "World" in John

It is important to have a good grasp on how John used the word *world* in his writings. He used the term more than all the New Testament writers together. Of the 185 times it appears in the New Testament, 105 occur in the writings of John (78 times in his Gospel, 24 times in his letters, 3 times in Revelation). John did not use "world" in only one way with only one clear definition. He appears to use it with a variety of meanings. Determining which meaning is used at any given time is an important matter for correct interpretation.

The Greek Word: *kosmos*

How John Uses the Word:

1. In reference to the universe at large (e.g., John 1:10; 8:12; 9:5).
2. In reference to the earth, the world in which we live (e.g., John 16:33; 1 John 4:17).
3. In reference to a large group or majority of people, somewhat as a hyperbole (e.g., John 12:19).

4. In reference to the whole race of sinful people who are in opposition to God (e.g., John 3:16; 1 John 2:2; 4:9).

5. In reference to the whole moral order of society organized under the powers of evil and in rebellion against God (John 14:30; 1 John 2:15–17; 5:19). There are no believers who are a part of the "world" in this sense. They have been rescued from the world (John 15:19). This is how John normally used *kosmos*.

The Command Not to Love (2:15a)

On the heels of the second test of life, the test of love, John commanded his readers not to love the world. The imperative "love" is from the same verb (*agape*) as in verses 9–11. How do we reconcile this prohibition with both the second test and Jesus' command to love our brothers, our neighbors, and even our enemies? The key is to understand what John referred to when he used the word *world* six different times in this paragraph. The "world" is the whole moral order of society organized under the powers of evil against God. We are to love the people in the world as God does (John 3:16), but we are commanded not to love the world's system or its ways. This becomes clear in verse 16 when the "world" is described.

Two Reasons for the Command (15a–17)

In verses 15a–17 John gave two reasons why his command should be heeded. The first reason is that love for the world and love for God are mutually exclusive. A person cannot do both. As John stated it, "If anyone loves the world, the love of the Father is not in him" (v. 15b). You cannot be involved in the ways of the world, which are in constant rebellion against God, and still love God.

Leon Morris gives a helpful hint about interpreting this word *kosmos* in John's Gospel that applies to all of John's writings. He writes, "The word thus has many shades of meaning. This diversity must be kept in mind in studying this Gospel, because the boundaries between the classifications are not hard-and-fast. John moves freely from one to another, or even uses the term in ways that may evoke more than one of its possible meanings" (Leon Morris, *The Gospel According to John*, 113).

"No one can serve two masters. Either he will hate the one and love the other, or he will be devoted to the one and despise the other. You cannot serve both God and Money" (Matt. 6:24). James also emphasized Jesus' point: "You adulterous people, don't you know that friendship with the world is hatred toward God? Anyone who chooses to be a friend of the world becomes an enemy of God" (James 4:4).

The Greek word for "sinful man" in verse 16 is *sarks*, which literally means "flesh." It can mean "the body," but it is the typical way of describing the sinful nature and is often contrasted with the Spirit-led life.

John used three concise statements in verse 16 to explain the major characteristics of "everything in the world." First, "the cravings of sinful man" describes the wrongful desires of our sinful nature. John described how the world's temptations begin from within us. Second, "the lust of his eyes" describes the wrongful desires that are inspired through our vision. The world tempts us by its physical attraction. Its ways appear good, but its beauty has no substance. Third, "the boasting of what he has and does" describes arrogance due to material possessions. Literally, this phrase is "the boasting of life," where "life" (*bios*) means life in its human or material form. In context, it refers to material possessions. The world's system encourages us to outshine others in wealth and possessions.

Believers should not love the world because the world is temporal and believers are eternal. John explained that the "world and its desires pass away" (17a). "Pass away" is the same verb in the same tense (present) as was used in verse 8 to describe the present downfall of the darkness. Here the "darkness" is described as the "world," and again John described it as in the process passing away. The assumption is when the world passes, those who are a part of it will pass too.

However, the opposite is also true. Whoever "does the will of God," or loves God, "lives forever" (17b). "Lives" translates a word that also means "remains/abides." This serves as a motivation to overcome the temptations of the world and not to love it. There can be no permanent satisfaction from anything in the world; it is all temporal. The only thing of permanent value is that associated with God and His will. As Williams translates, "He who perseveres in doing God's will lives on forever" (Charles B. Williams, *The New Testament in the Language of the People*).

- Christians are characterized by their love.
- However, a true believer is selective in the
- object of his or her love. You cannot love both
- God and the world because they are mutu-
- ally exclusive realities and because the world
- is temporal and believers are eternal. John
- declared, "Be in the world, but don't love it."

QUESTIONS TO GUIDE YOUR STUDY

1. What are the primary differences between the church and the "world"?
2. What did John mean when he said, "the Word of God lives in you"?
3. Why can a Christian not love both God and the world? Does this ring true to you? Why?

THE DOCTRINAL TEST: A CALL TO RIGHT BELIEF (2:18–27)

John now returned to his major purpose—to show the difference between false and true believers. He moved to his third test—the doctrinal test, the test of belief. He presented this by distinguishing between the heretics and the true believers (vv. 18–21), by describing their wrong teaching (vv. 22–23), and by giving safeguards to prevent wrong belief (vv. 24–27).

The Difference between the Heretics and the True Believers (2:18–21)

John began by stating with confidence that they were living in the "last hour," which in essence means the final days before the Second Coming of Christ. He then gave evidence that this is the last hour by describing the events which signify

John and the other New Testament writers viewed Christ's incarnation as the beginning of the beginning of the end, the inauguration of the "last days" or the "new age." Here John claimed that the "last hour" has come. Though there are numerous opinions about what this means, it appears that he spoke of the period before Christ's return that is marked by a last surge of the evil forces against His kingdom.

The New Testament church believed that the coming of the Antichrist, the personal embodiment of evil, would be a hallmark of the resurgence of evil that would precede the Second Coming of Christ. These "antichrists" around John's churches were not "the Antichrist," but, they manifested his spirit.

John demonstrated two important doctrines of the church. The first is the perseverance of the saints, which teaches that those who are truly saved will remain true to Christ until the end. It is not endurance that saves but endurance is the characteristic of the truly saved. The second is the doctrine of the true church, which teaches that only those who are true to Christ are members of the church and only Christ really knows who that is. Remember, a time is coming when who we really are will be revealed by the honest and clear vision of Christ. Are you a member of the true church or do you just give the appearance of membership? Time will tell.

it. Finally, he described the life of the true believers.

The evidence ("this is how we know," v. 18) that the "last hour" is here was the appearance of "antichrists." The appearance of the Antichrist was long thought to be a sign of the approaching end. The believers around Ephesus knew of this teaching because it was a part of the apostolic teaching they received (2 Thess. 2:5). For John, the "many antichrists" (v. 18) are forerunners of the Antichrist still to come. In 1 John 4:3, he spoke of the "spirit of the antichrist" which is now in the world.

These antichrists were not evil spiritual creatures but false teachers. John unmasked their identity in verse 19, and they were probably the same as the "false prophets" of 4:1. These "antichrists" revealed their true colors when they left the believers ("went out"). This is the same verb that described Judas' departure from the disciples on the night of his betrayal (John 13:30; "he went out").

John drew a sharp distinction between the heretics and the true believers. Their going proved that they never really belonged to the community of faith, although they had a superficial connection. John was so convinced of this that he could write, "For if they had belonged to us, they would have remained with us" (v. 19b).

In verses 20 and 21, John gave assurance to the true believers in the church, the ones who remained after the antichrists left. Their assurance comes from two things.

First, they "have an anointing from the Holy One" (v. 20). The "Holy One" could be a title designating either God or Christ. The "anointing" probably refers to the giving of the Holy Spirit to believers as Christ Himself was anointed not with oil, but by the Holy Spirit at His baptism (Luke 4:18; Acts 4:27; 10:38). The antichrists were against Christ and were falsely claiming to be like Him, while the true believers were truly like Him and were striving to be for Him. The personal pronoun "you" is emphatic, emphasizing John's confidence in their salvation.

Second, John's readers could have assurance because they "know the truth" (v. 20). This thought is elaborated in verse 27. Here we should make the connection between the Holy Spirit and truth. John had taught that the Holy Spirit, the "Spirit of truth" (John 14:17), would become their teacher (John 14:26). John claimed that all the readers have "knowledge" because they have all received the "anointing," the Holy Spirit. In verse 21 he stated that he was writing them to give them this assurance.

Jesus received the title the "Holy One" in the New Testament. "'You do not want to leave too, do you?' Jesus asked the Twelve. Simon Peter answered him, 'Lord, to whom shall we go? You have the words of eternal life. We believe and know that you are the Holy One of God'" (John 6:67–69).

■ *The "last hour" is here, but John didn't want*
■ *his readers to panic. They could see that they*
■ *were different from the heretics and, there-*
■ *fore, could find assurance. Their reception of*
■ *the Holy Spirit and his teaching them of truth*
■ *firmly established them as different from the*
■ *antichrists.*

The Explanation and Effects of the Heresy (2:22–23)

The false teaching of those who left the church is revealed in these verses. They denied that Jesus is the Christ. These teachers must have taught a false doctrine similar to full-blown

Paul gave similar assurance to the church in Corinth. He wrote, "Now it is God who makes both us and you stand firm in Christ. He anointed us, set his seal of ownership on us, and put his Spirit in our hearts as a deposit, guaranteeing what is to come" (2 Cor. 1:21–22).

Many "religions" and cults can be singled out as carrying the spirit of the Antichrist and as being wrong in their belief system simply by checking their doctrine about the character of Jesus. Do not be deceived. Any group which does not believe that Jesus is the Christ, the Son of God, is not in right relationship with the Father.

Paul summarized saving faith in the words of confession also. He wrote, "That if you confess with your mouth, 'Jesus is Lord,' and believe in your heart that God raised him from the dead, you will be saved. For it is with your heart that you believe and are justified, and it is with your mouth that you confess and are saved" (Rom. 10:9–10).

Gnosticism of the second century. Some of the Gnostics said that Jesus, the man, was not the same as Christ, the divine being. To them, Christ was only united with Jesus the man during a portion of His earthly ministry. Therefore, Jesus was not the Christ. He was just a man. The incarnation wasn't real.

John made the standard for this test of belief clear. He had already declared, that one who disobeys God's commands or hates his brother but claims to know God is a "liar" (1:6; 2:4). The same is true in this third test for the person who believes this heresy and denies that Jesus is the Christ. The basic doctrinal test for salvation is one's belief about who Jesus is. To deny His deity and His humanity is not just a wrong belief; it is a belief that eliminates one from the family of God. John was direct: "Such a man is the antichrist" (v. 22)—one of those who exemplify the spirit of the Antichrist to come.

The effects of belief are described clearly in verses 22c–23. The one who "acknowledges" Jesus is in relationship with both the Father and the Son. John must have had in mind a public denial and acknowledgment since he used the same two verbs that Jesus used on the same subject (Matt. 10:32–33). Of course, inward belief precedes public acknowledgment.

■ *To buy into the belief that Jesus is not the*
■ *Christ is to reject a saving relationship with*
■ *the Father and His Son.*

Protection against the Heresy (2:24–27)
John next exhorted his readers to protect themselves from falling prey to the false teaching.

They could do so by remaining true to the apostolic teaching and the heavenly teacher.

He first commanded them to let the original gospel message, the apostolic teaching, "remain in" them. This is described as "what you have heard from the beginning" (v. 24a). The Greek begins with an emphatic "you" (as does verse 27). This was John's way of setting the readers over against the heretics. John assumes they must work to keep the apostolic teaching a part of their lives. They must not allow themselves to be caught up in false ideas and incorrect doctrines. If they kept apostolic teaching a part of their lives, then they would "remain in the Son and in the Father" (v. 24b), which is simply another description of "eternal life" (v. 25).

Next John commanded believers to let the Holy Spirit, "the anointing," remain in them (v. 27).

They had "heard" (v. 24a) the apostolic teaching from the apostles, and they had "received" the Holy Spirit "from him" (v. 27). This referred to the Holy One, Jesus Christ. Both were means of staying true to the Lord.

John provided his readers with two forms of protection: the truth of the Word and the Spirit of truth. John claimed that they needed to remain in both. He reminded all of his readers of this important balance. A person should not focus on the Scripture over against the Spirit or vice versa. What John claimed is that the best safeguard against false teaching is a real knowledge of the truth as gained through study and Spirit-guided illumination.

"For the time will come when men will not put up with sound doctrine. Instead, to suit their own desires, they will gather around them a great number of teachers to say what their itching ears want to hear. They will turn their ears away from the truth and turn aside to myths" (2 Tim. 4:3).

Remember, "eternal life" in John's writings is not so much about time as it is about a quality of life. It begins with salvation and crosses through death into all eternity. It is seen as union with God and Christ (1 John 2:24–25) and knowing God and Christ (John 17:3).

Emphatically stating that true believers had the Holy Spirit (the personal pronoun "you" is placed at the front of the sentence in Greek), John commanded them to remain in Him.

John Calvin on Scripture and the Holy Spirit

"Therefore Scripture will ultimately suffice for a saving knowledge of God only when its certainty is founded upon the inward persuasion of the Holy Spirit" (*Institutes*, I, vii, 5).

■ *It is the Word of God and the Holy Spirit's*
■ *illumination of that word that will keep a*
■ *person true to the heavenly Father. The*
■ *proper understanding and application of*
■ *Scriptures is the key to a person's security in*
■ *the Lord.*

This ends the first set of three tests that John offered. There are two more sets coming. He gave his readers assurance and stole the assurance of the false teachers by guiding his readers to the revealing tests of obedience, love, and belief.

QUESTIONS TO GUIDE YOUR STUDY

1. Who is "the Antichrist" and how do "antichrists" differ from him?

2. Is the "anointing" only for certain believers? Does John teach that the Holy Spirit is received more than once?

3. What are the two forms of protection against heretical teachings that John gave? How do they work together?

THE SECOND APPLICATION OF THE TESTS OF LIFE (2:28–4:6)

John now circled back for a second look at each of his three tests. With each new look came a more solid affirmation of the tests' validity as well as a further development of the idea behind it. John looked again at the test of obedience (2:28–3:10), the test of love (3:11–18), and the test of belief (4:1–6). In between the second and third test, he inserted an aside about assurance and the condemning heart (3:19–24).

A new topic should be noticed at this point. John introduced an idea in verse 29 that permeates the rest of this letter. It is the idea of believers being "born" of God and, therefore, being children of God. While "fellowship" has dominated the letter up to this point, "family relationship" carries the thought from here on out. Paul used similar language, but he emphasized sonship and, therefore, adoption. John focused on believers as children (he never used *sons*) and, therefore, regeneration.

A SECOND LOOK AT THE TEST OF OBEDIENCE (2:28–3:10)

John took a second look at the moral test of obedience. He now framed the test with the standard of "righteousness" and the call to do "what is right." A form of the word *appearing* occurs six times in these verses, signifying John's method. He motivated the believers to obey Christ because of Christ's two appearances: His future appearance (2:28–3:3) and His past appearance (3:4–10).

Motivation to Obedience from Christ's Future Appearance (2:28–3:3)

John mentioned the Second Coming of Christ as a motivation to "continue in him" (v. 28a) before he discussed the test of obedience (vv. 29–3:3). The phrases in verse 28 translated "when he appears" and "coming" are clear references to Christ's future appearance. John encouraged believers to stay in relationship with Christ for two reasons related to this Second Coming.

The first reason we should continue in Christ is so "we may be confident" (v. 28b) when He

The two Greek words translated "appear" and "coming" have some interesting meanings that help describe Christ's Second Coming. The word for "appear" suggests an unveiling, an uncovering, a revealing, or manifestation. Christ and His glory are now hidden in some degree as He resides at the Father's right hand. At His future appearance, He and His glory will be revealed. The word for "coming" (used only here by John, but often by Paul) is a technical term for a royal visit. It describes Christ's Second Coming into the presence of His people.

returns. This word means "freedom of speech" or "outspokenness." Used in this context, it means boldness, courage, unreserved confidence. It portrays dramatically the freedom from inhibitions that Christ desires us to have as we approach Him now (see Heb. 4:16; 10:19) and in His future coming.

The second reason we should continue in Jesus is so we may be "unashamed" (v. 28b) when He returns. This phrase may more literally be translated "and not be shamed away from Him." Those who have not remained in Him will instinctively shrink away from Him at His Second Coming with feelings of guilt and disgrace. Both of these motivations should spur the reader on to obedience.

Jesus vividly portrayed the judgment of His Second Coming in the parable of the wedding banquet. Here we see a person who lacks confidence. "But when the king came in to see the guests, he noticed a man there who was not wearing wedding clothes. 'Friend,' he asked, 'how did you get in here without wedding clothes?' The man was speechless. Then the king told the attendants, 'Tie him hand and foot, and throw him outside, into the darkness, where there will be weeping and gnashing of teeth'" (Matt. 22:11–13).

John now held out the test of obedience for a second time (2:29–3:3). Doing "what is right" (v. 29) is the mark of a true believer. This standard is based upon the character of Christ and God. John used two different words for "know" to explain the test. The first "know" is a word for intuition (knowing as a matter of fact). The second "know" refers to experiential knowledge or perception. If you know for a fact that He is righteous, then you can perceive that those who do right are "born of him." The character of the Father is revealed in the child. Knowledge is not the best indicator of the regenerated. A righteous life of obedience is the true test.

The mention of this new "birth" caused John to cry out in wonder at God's gift. In the first three verses of chapter 3, he described what it means to be a child of God.

Five ideas summarize John's thoughts on what it means to be a child of God: (1) We are recipients of God's love (v. 1a); (2) we are true children, not just titlebearers (v. 1b); (3) we do not know for sure the full glory of our future destiny (v. 2a); (4) we will ultimately be conformed to Christ's image (v. 2b); and (5) we will some day be face to face with God (v. 2c).

From these incredible truths related to Christ's Second Coming, John again saw motivation to obey Him. The proposition that we will see and be like Christ some day is a powerful incentive to grow in conformity to Him now. John said, "Everyone who has this hope in him purifies himself, just as he is pure" (v. 3). The person who has the confident expectation of seeing Christ at His Second Coming naturally gets ready. To *purify* means "to put away all that defiles," and in context it specifically relates to moral sins. Although Christ's work is the only thing that can purify us completely (1 John 1:7), we have a responsibility to seek to purify ourselves on a daily basis (see 2 Cor. 7:1; 1 Tim. 5:22; James 4:8).

Have you ever lacked confidence or felt too ashamed to pray to God because of your lack of obedience? If we feel that way now in our prayers, imagine what it will be like when we stand face to face with Almighty God. Maybe we, too, should be motivated by His Second Coming to obey Him now.

■ *The test is the moral one. The standard is the*
■ *righteous and pure Christ Himself. The moti-*
■ *vation is the fact that we will see Him and He*
■ *will see us. The natural correlation is that*
■ *true believers should live a righteous and*
■ *pure life.*

Motivation to Obedience from Christ's Past Appearance (3:4–10)

The motivation to live a life of obedience is now linked to the past appearance of Christ. In the previous verses, the motivation was from the expected return of Christ. Now it is from the first coming of Christ. Since He came to remove

The phrase translated "how great" (3:1) comes from one Greek word (*potapen*). Originally the word meant "of what country" and came to mean "of what sort." John recognized that the Father's love is so "unearthly," so "out of this world," that he wondered from where it came. God's love is unlike anything else in this world.

"God made him who had no sin to be sin for us, so that in him we might become the righteousness of God" (2 Cor. 5:21; See also Heb. 7:26; 1 Pet. 1:19; 2:22).

sins, a righteous life is required from those who are united with Him. The argument is presented twice in these seven verses with a slightly different angle in each. The first discusses the nature of sin and the second the origin of it. Both call the believer to moral obedience. Notice the similarities (adapted from Stott, 125):

	VERSES 4–7	VERSES 8–10
THE INTRODUCTORY PHRASE	"Everyone who sins" (v. 4).	"He who does what is sinful" (v. 8).
THE THEME	The nature of sin is lawlessness.	The origin of sin is the devil.
THE PURPOSE OF CHRIST'S APPEARING	"He might take away our sins" (v. 5).	"to destroy the devil's work" (v. 8).
THE LOGICAL CONCLUSION	"No one who lives in him keeps on sinning" (v. 6).	"No one who is born of God will continue to sin" (v. 9).

The Nature of Sin (3:4–7)

John first defined the nature of sin by stating a universal principle: "Everyone who sins breaks the law" (v. 4a). The present tense behind "sins" (v. 3) suggests the doing of sin as a practice, not the committing of an individual act of sin.

The root meaning of sin (*hamartia*) is "missing the mark." "Lawlessness" (*anomia*) suggests defiance or rebellion against God's moral law. It denotes the attitude or spirit of a person that prompts sinful actions.

John then defined sin: "Sin is lawlessness" (v. 4b). He indicated the two are equal. Sin does not *result* in rebellion against God; sin *is* rebellion against God and His will.

John next showed how sin is contrary to Christ and His work. His appearing and His incarnation had a purpose: "so that he might take away our sins" (v. 5). "Take away" has the meaning of "to lift" or "to carry" and may mean to take away by bearing. It is our "sins" (plural) that Christ came to take away, where in John 1:29 it is our "sin" (singular). The plural may suggest the fruit of the singular root. Probably in both places, expiation and sanctification are meant. Christ was able to do this because "in him is no sin."

The logical conclusion is that the person living in sin cannot be associated with Christ and the person associated with Christ will not be living a life of sin (v. 6). With a broad brush, John declared that true believers do not have sin as the ruling principle of their lives. If it is, then they are not true believers. John did not contradict himself. He knew that believers commit sinful acts (1:8), but they do not live sinful lifestyles.

John concluded this thought with a strong warning: Righteousness is important. "Do not let anyone lead you astray," (v. 7a) he warned. You cannot be righteous without practicing righteousness. Our nature is shown in our actions.

The Origin of Sin (3:8–10)

Where does sin come from? The person habitually practicing sin is "of the devil." The one who sins has the devil as his father. Sin is characteristic of the devil. He has been sinning since the beginning of his rebellious state and is still sinning. The person who sins shows who his father is.

Jesus came in His incarnation "to destroy the devil's work" (v. 8b). The Greek word for "to destroy" (*luo*) means "to loose," "to release," " to break." Christ is pictured as having come in His first appearance in order to break the bondage of sin and sin's effects in our lives.

A fully defined doctrine of Satan does not appear in the Old Testament, though when he does appear he is always the adversary of God and His people. The New Testament authors gave a more clear-cut doctrine of Satan. The origin of evil is within Satan, and he has fallen angels or demons assisting him in his work. Jesus was tempted by Satan, and Paul referred to him as the god of this age. Satin is a creature, so he is always in subordination to God. He was defeated by Christ at the cross, but God has allowed him to work until Christ returns. Although he poses a great threat to all people, Jesus promised we would never be tempted by him in such a way that we couldn't resist.

John did not deny that true believers may sin occasionally. He denied that people with a sinful lifestyle can be true believers. Sinful acts are often a part of a true believer's life, but sinful lifestyles are never a part of a believer's life. The true believer hates sin and diligently resists it settling into his or her life.

The logical conclusion is found in verse 9 in the form of a universal principle. The true believer, the one "born of God," will not "continue to sin" or "go on sinning." Again, as in verse 6, these are both present tense verbs denoting a continual and habitual lifestyle of sin.

"His divine power has given us everything we need for life and godliness through our knowledge of him who called us by his own glory and goodness. Through these he has given us his very great and precious promises, so that through them you may participate in the divine nature and escape the corruption in the world caused by evil desires" (2 Pet. 1:3–4).

Why is this true? John answered with two causal statements in verse 9: "because God's seed remains in him" and "because he has been born of God." These two phrases are parallel. "God's seed" is John's way of saying God's nature. The person born of God has received God's divine nature as a mark of his or her new birth. This new nature works from within believers to transform them—conforming them to Christ. If a person lives a lifestyle of sin, then it is obvious that the new nature is not a part of his or her life. He or she is not a true believer. Verse 10 is a transition summarizing and concluding the above discussion while paving the way for the social test of love.

■ *John restated the moral test as "doing right"*
■ *and gave the motivation based upon Christ's*
■ *past appearance. How a person measures up*
■ *in that test lands him in one of two camps.*
■ *There is no middle ground. You are either a*
■ *child of the devil or a child of God. Whose*
■ *you are is evident in how you live.*

QUESTIONS TO GUIDE YOUR STUDY

1. In what way is the Second Coming of Christ a motivation for obedience in the present?

2. What did John mean when he said someone has been "born of him" (2:29)?

3. What is the nature of sin and the origin of sin? How can they motivate you to obedience?

A SECOND LOOK AT THE TEST OF LOVE (3:11–18)

John is now ready to lead his readers into a second look at the second test. Having shown them a preliminary outline of the test of love in 2:7–11, he distinguished between the hatred of the world exemplified in Cain (3:12–13) and the love of believers exemplified in Christ (3:14–18).

The Message of Love (3:11)

The old-new command of chapter 2 was the command to love. Here "the message you heard from the beginning" is made emphatically clear. The love commanded is both mutual and reciprocal. There is no target mentioned. It is a love for all people.

The Hatred of the World (3:12–13)

To contrast love with hate, John drew an illustration from the world's second generation. In the conflict between Cain and Abel, we see the awful consequences of anger, hate, and making wrong choices. Cain's murderous act revealed his family of origin. He "belonged to the evil one" (v. 12). His jealousy turned into hatred. Hatred resulted in murder. In this deed, his identity was revealed.

Based upon the truth behind this real-life illustration, a command is given (v. 13). Believers are not to be surprised if the world hates them. Why? Because hatred is all the world knows. Cain's life is simply a picture of how the world works. Children of the devil act like the devil, and the people of the world hate like their "father."

"In the course of time Cain brought some of the fruits of the soil as an offering to the LORD. But Abel brought fat portions from some of the firstborn of his flock. The LORD looked with favor on Abel and his offering, but on Cain and his offering he did not look with favor. So Cain was very angry, and his face was downcast. Then the LORD said to Cain, 'Why are you angry? Why is your face downcast? If you do what is right, will you not be accepted? But if you do not do what is right, sin is crouching at your door; it desires to have you, but you must master it.' Now Cain said to his brother Abel, 'Let's go out to the field.' And while they were in the field, Cain attacked his brother Abel and killed him" (Gen. 4:3–8).

The Love of Believers (3:14–18)

The contrast between true believers and people of the world is now presented. What do loving attitudes prove about a person (vv. 14–15)? What does love look like (vv. 16–18)?

A life of love is an indication that a person is saved. "We know" means that John and the true believers *know* for a fact. What they know is that they are saved from death. The classic picture of salvation is painted here by John when he refers to the passing "from death to life" (v. 14). The perfect tense of the verb *passed* signifies an act accomplished in the past with the results remaining in the present. "Life," meaning eternal life, is the permanent state of the believer that came about as an act of faith.

"We have passed" translates a picturesque Greek word (*metabaino*). It is normally used of a topographical change of place. For example, it is translated "leave" in John 7:3: "You ought to leave here and go to Judea." In John 13:1, Jesus used it to describe His departure from this world to go to the Father. When used of "passing" from death to life, a literal spiritual change of address is meant. Jesus taught this reality when He said, "I tell you the truth, whoever hears my word and believes him who sent me has eternal life and will not be condemned; he has crossed over from death to life" (John 5:24).

The opposite is also true. The person without love is still in death. The present tense of the verb *remains* (v. 14b) signifies the current and abiding position of the person who does not love. The reason for this condition is stated in verse 15. The person who lives a lifestyle of hatred is essentially a murderer and does not possess eternal life.

John is finally ready to give some substance to his teaching on love. Here in verses 16–18, he defined love by way of example. No longer is this a vague command but a specific duty.

John began by writing literally: "In this we know love" (v. 16a). "We know" translates the word for *know* that means to "know by experience." How do we come to understand the nature of love? It was not possible to grasp this until Christ had "laid down his life for us" (v. 16b). He sacrificed His physical life for us. This is love. As Cain was the supreme example of hate, Christ is the perfect picture of love. To rob a person of his or her life (murder) is the worst of sins. To give up one's life for another is the supreme example of love.

John quickly turned from the definition to the response. He focused on the example, and then pointed the way toward action. If love is the mark of a true believer, and if love is defined by Christ's laying down His life for us, then "we ought to lay down our lives for our brothers" (v. 16c). The effects of Christ's loving self-sacrifice are unique, but the pattern for our social behavior is set by Him. We must sacrifice for others.

If John's readers thought that death is the only way to love others, he reminded them in verses 17–18 that love is eminently practical. John switched the target of love from plural ("our brothers," v. 16) to singular ("his brother," v. 17). By doing so, he brought the command from the world of theory to the world of practical and attainable action. True believers love by sharing what they have with those who are in need. If they don't, "how can the love of God be in them?"

"Your attitude should be the same as that of Christ Jesus: Who, being in very nature God, did not consider equality with God something to be grasped, but made himself nothing, taking the very nature of a servant, being made in human likeness. And being found in appearance as a man, he humbled himself and became obedient to death—even death on a cross!" (Phil. 2:5–8).

■ *The world is characterized by hatred that*
■ *comes from the devil. Such hatred produces*
■ *murder, proving their existence in spiritual*
■ *death. The true believer is characterized by*
■ *love that comes from the Father. This pro-*
■ *duces self-sacrifice and proves their exist-*
■ *ence in eternal life.*

QUESTIONS TO GUIDE YOUR STUDY

1. What does it mean to *hate* someone? Can hate be a part of a Christian's life?

2. What does it mean to "lay down our lives for our brothers?"

3. How did John enhance his teaching on love in this test as compared to the first one?

AN ASIDE ABOUT ASSURANCE AND THE CONDEMNING HEART (3:19–24)

This passage is an "aside," but it is important. Verses 19–20 relate how assurance is gained, and verses 21–24 describe some benefits of this assurance.

How Assurance Is Gained (3:19–20)

Two types of assurance are described here: (1) the assurance that comes in normal times and (2) the assurance that is needed in times of crisis when our own hearts condemn us. In both cases the assurance comes from the same source. "This is how" points backward towards the truth that love toward others carried through in actions is proof of a person's true relationship with Christ. It is this genuine love that provides the assurance that "we belong to the truth."

The phrase "set at rest" translates a unique word in the New Testament (*peisomen*). It only occurs here and in Matt. 28:14. The basic meaning of the word is "to convince" or "to persuade." In context it takes on the meaning of "pacify," "soothe," or "reassure." As a tranquilizer can calm a wild animal, so the truth can pacify a confused heart.

The crisis John brought up is the crisis of a condemning heart. The phrase "whenever our hearts condemn us" in verse 20 reveals that this may not be such an abnormal or infrequent crisis. When it does occur, it is a continual, persistent work of our conscience. At times the true believer may experience thoughts which encourage doubt.

When this happens, John says there is a way in which assurance can be gained, a way in which our hearts can be "set at rest." In those moments when doubt enters a believer's heart, it is not the feelings that are to be trusted; it is knowledge. What we know about the truth and our compliance with it can bring assurance. If there is evidence of a sacrificial, loving lifestyle, then assurance is gained. This kind of love is not natural; it is bred into those who have become God's children. So the visible evidence of Christlike love produces the assurance of a Christ-saved life.

Our hearts or our consciences cannot always be trusted. John declared, "God is greater than our hearts, and he knows everything." God is greater in that He is more knowledgeable and is more true. Sometimes our hearts will condemn us, but if a true believer is condemned, then the accusations are unjust and we are to rely on the justice and mercy of God.

The Benefits of Assurance (3:21–24)

John moved into the wonderful benefits of assurance with a term of endearment. With the title "dear friends" (literally "beloved"), the heaviness of his discussion lightens somewhat and the freshness of relief is felt. John listed two benefits of assurance (vv. 21–22) and gave a summary of God's commands (v. 23) before he gave his final thought on assurance (v. 24).

Two primary benefits of assurance are mentioned in verses 21–22. First, there is "confidence before God." John mentioned this confidence in 2:28 in the context of the believer before Christ at the Second Coming of Christ. Here he said this can be a present experience. The principle is that the true believer obeys the love command and has confidence to speak boldly before God.

The second benefit is the assurance of answered prayer: "And receive from him anything we ask" (v. 22a). "Ask" and "receive" are both in the present tense, suggesting an ongoing activity and experience of immediate response by God

Paul spoke about the reverse effect of his conscience. He said that even though his conscience did not condemn him, he didn't trust it. He felt that we could be led astray by our hearts' silence into a false assurance. He wrote, "My conscience is clear, but that does not make me innocent. It is the Lord who judges me" (1 Cor. 4:4).

The process of salvation is an objective event. When people truly trust in the Christ who actually died for their sins, then they "will be saved" (Rom. 10:9). Whether a person feels saved or not is never the issue. Assurance is never based upon subjective standards; it rests upon objective facts. Our feelings or conscience can prompt us to investigate the facts. Never ask yourself or anyone else if they feel saved. Ask if you have done what the Scriptures teach in order to be saved. Look for the evidence that John speaks about in this letter. Feelings are not one of the tests of salvation.

John reflected his earlier writing where Jesus taught, "If you remain in me and my words remain in you, ask whatever you wish, and it will be given you" (John 15:7).

to our prayers. There is a condition for such a benefit (not a cause). This condition is that the believers "obey his commands and do what pleases him" (v. 22b). This obedience and pleasing action (namely to love others) are evidence that our will is in harmony with God's. God doesn't just grant whatever a believer asks. He gives when the prayer is asked according to His will (1 John 5:14).

What are the commands that we are to obey? John gave them in verse 23, but he listed them only as one command (note the singular, "command") with two parts. First, we are to "believe in the name of his Son, Jesus Christ." To believe in the name means "to accept the character of." We are commanded to believe that the man Jesus is the Messiah, the Christ who is the Son of God. The verb *believe* is in the aorist tense, and signifies a single, once-for-all act. Second, we are "to love one another as he commanded us." "To love" translates a present-tense verb that signifies ongoing, continual action. Faith and love are combined into a single command. Obedience of this command keeps the believer in the heart of God's will.

In verse 24, John added that the Spirit aids in our assurance. John's mention of the Spirit does not introduce a new inward or subjective test. John is saying that the Spirit in us is the one who can lead us to obey, love, and believe. Therefore, assurance comes as we look for and find evidence of the Holy Spirit in our lives.

■ *An unsettled heart in a believer can be*
■ *soothed by understanding what the Scrip-*
■ *tures teach about a believer's lifestyle and*
■ *comparing that standard to his or her own*
■ *life. True assurance is a wonderful thing that*
■ *gives confidence to pray and receive*
■ *answers.*

QUESTIONS TO GUIDE YOUR STUDY

1. How do you think our hearts become unsettled in the first place?
2. What is the key to receiving answered prayers?
3. How can a person pray in God's will?

A SECOND LOOK AT THE TEST OF BELIEF (4:1–6)

The readers of this letter were members of a church in controversy. The opponents whom John was engaging were not professed pagans but people who claimed to be Christians. They had the intellectual ammunition to be persuasive. Their effect on the church was to lead other people astray and to plant doubt in authentic believers.

In this type of setting, John needed to teach his readers how to discern between true and false teachers. He explained to them that the content of their teaching is the test of the teachers' authenticity (vv. 1–3). He then explained that the character of the listeners is a test of their authenticity (vv. 4–6).

The Content of the Teaching (4:1–3)

After explaining what we should believe (3:23), John focused on what we should not believe. There is no such thing as "blind faith" for a true

With the words "do not believe every spirit" (4:1), John brought his readers into a world with which they were familiar. Perhaps many people today are not aware of this world. The church services of the apostolic period were much more free and "spiritual" than is true of many churches today. The structure was less formal and less rigid. Many different people participated in the service. Anyone was free to address the congregation. In such an atmosphere, false teaching could easily be established.

Spirit comes from a word that can mean "wind" or "spirit." It is the same word used for the Holy Spirit. What did John mean by "spirit" in this passage? He spoke about a superhuman spirit that lies behind the human teacher. Behind every human is some spirit (either the Holy Spirit or an evil spirit), and behind every spirit is his head (either God or the devil). John indicated that we should test the spirit behind the teacher "to see whether they are from God" (v. 1b).

Jesus warned about false prophets. "Watch out for false prophets. They come to you in sheep's clothing, but inwardly they are ferocious wolves" (Matt. 7:15). Paul also warned of their coming. "I know that after I leave, savage wolves will come in among you and will not spare the flock. Even from your own number men will arise and distort the truth in order to draw away disciples after them. So be on your guard!" (Acts 20:29–31a). Peter also gave a warning. "But there were also false prophets among the people, just as there will be false teachers among you. They will secretly introduce destructive heresies, even denying the sovereign Lord who brought them" (2 Pet. 2:1)

believer. The object of our faith is to be carefully chosen. We have the Holy Spirit in us, but there are other spirits in this world. We are commanded: "Do not believe every spirit, but test the spirits" (4:1).

The testing of the spirits was necessary because many "false prophets have gone out into the world" (v. 1c). A prophet was someone who spoke a message more than someone who foretold the future. Many who appeared as prophets were actually "false prophets" (*pseudoprophetai*). These are equated with the "many antichrists" of 2:18–19.

How do you test the spirits? Verses 2–3 answer that question. It is a test of belief. The authenticity of the spirit can be discerned from the words of the teacher.

The content of correct doctrine is narrowed to one simple truth, found in what a person "acknowledges" (v. 2). To acknowledge means "to confess openly and publicly." The Spirit from God leads a person to acknowledge that "Jesus Christ has come in the flesh" (v. 2). This simple phrase carries the essential elements of Christian faith. It is the test of what one believes about Jesus. The correct belief involves acceptance of Jesus as the preexistent, incarnate Christ.

This is the crucial doctrinal test. In order to be a God-given, Spirit-led confession, the substance of the confession must have the right perspective on Jesus Christ. To make sure he was understood, John states the opposite in verse 3a: "Every spirit that does not acknowledge Jesus is not from God." He shortened the phrase, but the substance of the confession is meant to be the same. These are not just false teachers. John called them the "spirit of the antichrist," and they are already in the world.

■ *To test the spirit of a teacher, you should*
■ *examine his or her teaching about Christ.*
■ *The true teacher will teach the truth about*
■ *Him: He is Jesus, the Christ, the Son of God.*

The Character of the Listeners (4:4–6)

John now turned from the content of the message to the character of the listeners. Each verse in this section begins with a different personal pronoun: "you" (plural, v. 4), "they" (v. 5), and "we" (v. 6), referring respectively to John's readers (i.e., true believers), the false prophets, and John as a representative of the apostles. He encouraged the readers in verse 4 and then applied the doctrinal test by way of the character of the listeners in verses 5–6.

John gave his readers assurance of their status with God: "You, dear children, are from God and have overcome them" (v. 4a). Earlier in verses 2–3 he maintained that the Spirit that passes the doctrinal test is "from God." Now he assured his readers that they, too, have passed this test and have overcome the false teachers. They have tested the spirits, found them to be false, and held to the proper doctrine. The perfect tense of "have overcome" is assuring, reflecting that the victory has come and the results will abide. This, no doubt, is why the false teachers "went out from" them (2:19).

The reason for their victory has nothing to do with their own abilities, but John credited "the one who is in" them (v. 4b). This must be a reference to the Holy Spirit (2:20, 27), who John

The confession of verse 2 countered Cerinthus's teaching that the Spirit of Christ only came on Jesus for a time. John declared He "has come" (a perfect tense) in the flesh. This means that the Incarnation is an abiding reality. God did come in the form of a man. His name is Jesus, and He is the Christ.

This is not a history lesson. The denial of the Jesus of history, who is also the eternal God, is a modern-day teaching as well. At the end of the twentieth century it is making its way into popular "Christian" books and interesting "Christian" sermons. It is doing so under the guise of scholarly credentials. You should be aware of this phenomenon. No matter how educated the teacher or how smooth the talker, if his or her doctrine teaches that Jesus Christ is someone other than God who entered history as a real person to save sinners, then he or she is a false teacher who serves an evil spirit.

A Christian's security is in the strength of God. Jesus said, "In this world you will have trouble. But take heart! I have overcome the world" (John 16:33). He also taught about the important ministry of the Holy Spirit. He said, "But the Counselor, the Holy Spirit, whom the Father will send in my name, will teach you all things and will remind you of everything I have said to you" (John 14:26).

John echoed the teaching of Jesus that he recorded in his Gospel. "He who belongs to God hears what God says. The reason you do not hear is that you do not belong to God" (John 8:47). "When he has brought out all his own, he goes on ahead of them, and his sheep follow him because they know his voice. But they will never follow a stranger; in fact, they will run away from him because they do not recognize a stranger's voice" (John 10:4–5).

identified later as the "Spirit of truth" (4:6). No matter how great "the one who is in the world" may be, the victory of the true believers is secure because the Holy Spirit is greater than the devil. The Spirit continues to illumine the apostolic teaching and help true believers discern false doctrine.

John turned from this strong word of encouragement to a strong contrast. In verses 5–6, he explained that the difference between true prophets and false prophets is not just the doctrine they teach but the character of those who listen to them. Verse 5 describes the false prophets ("they"), and verse 6 describes the apostolic teachers ("we") before John made a concluding remark.

The false prophets and the true teachers differ in origin and content of their teaching, but one key to recognizing who they are is to identify the character of their audience. The people of the world—those not born of God—listen to the false prophets. They like what they hear from them. However, those who know God, the true believers, listen to the apostolic message.

Originally, the doctrinal test was about content. Do you accept that "Jesus Christ has come in the flesh" (v. 2)? Now the doctrine is tested by whether it is accepted by Christians and rejected by non-Christians. The people of God will listen to the Word of God while the people of the world will not. True believers have the Holy Spirit to encourage and help them listen, while those in the world do not. "This is how we recognize the Spirit of truth and the spirit of falsehood" (v. 6b).

- Not only is a true "spirit" recognized by the
- content of the teaching, but they are also rec-
- ognized by the character of their audience.
- True believers listen to true doctrine, and
- false believers listen to false doctrine.

QUESTIONS TO GUIDE YOUR STUDY

1. What did John mean by "spirits" and the call to "test the spirits?"
2. What test would you give to see if a teacher is of God or of the devil?
3. How would you go about using the test concerning the character of the listeners?

THE THIRD APPLICATION OF THE TESTS OF LIFE (4:7–5:5)

So far John has presented two rounds of tests that help establish the authenticity of a believer. He has twice presented the three tests in order: the test of obedience (2:3–6; 2:28–3:10), the test of love (2:7–11; 3:11–18), and the test of belief (2:18–27; 4:1–6). With each new presentation, he has both elaborated and deepened the requirements of the test. Along with the tests themselves, he has put forward a call for each true believer to find assurance and to move forward in the application of these truths to their lives.

John is now ready to present the third round of the tests. This time the order is different and the strategy is altered. Following the command within the "aside" at 3:23 ("to believe . . . and to love"), John presented the second test of belief

"And now these three remain: faith, hope and love. But the greatest of these is love" (1 Cor. 13:13).

in 4:1–6. Now, with a new round of tests, instead of beginning again with the test of obedience, he quickly turned to the test of love (4:7–11) as commanded in 3:23. John then presented a combination of the tests of love and belief (4:12–21) before combining all three tests at the beginning of chapter 5. The switch in order underscores the greatest commandment: to love.

A CONCLUDING CALL TO LOVE (4:7–12)

This is perhaps the most loved and best known portion of John's letter. It is a glorious statement about *agape* love, but its order is somewhat difficult to follow. However, the phrase "love one another" in its various forms holds the passage together. It is used as an appeal (vv. 7–10), as an obligation (v. 11), and finally as the substance of the test of true relationship with God (v. 12).

The Appeal to Love (4:7–10)

Keep in mind what John meant when he used the term *know* in its various forms. He usually referred to an intimate relationship with God. Many people know a lot about God, but they don't know Him personally. Many people study a lot of books and memorize a lot of verses about God, but they spend little or no time with God. Christianity is not about religious knowledge; it is about an intimate, abiding relationship.

John began his concluding call to love with a tender but urgent appeal. He abruptly ended his former discussion and stated "Dear friends" (literally, "beloved"), "let us love one another" (v. 7). The present tense of this appeal reflects the call to a continual mutual love.

The difference between this and John's original calls to mutual love (3:11, 23) is the basis he gave for such an appeal. Here he listed two reasons for carrying out this call. First, God is the source and origin of love. John said it this way, "For love comes from God" (v. 7b). If God is the source of real love, then all who exemplify love in their lives must have gotten it from God. Thus, love becomes a test of a person's relationship with God: "Everyone who loves has been born of God and knows God" (v. 7c).

The opposite is also true. The person who does not have a lifestyle of love proves he or she does not know God. The change of tense in the verb *know* is important. In verse 7c it is present, signifying a relationship that is both intimate and continuing. The tense in verse 8a is not present, but aorist (past). It underscores the reality that the unloving person has never known God. Regardless of what a person says, if love is not the controlling principle of his or her life, he or she has have never known the source of love: God Himself.

John gave his second reason or basis for his appeal to love one another in the brief phrase at the end of verse 8: "God is love." This is one of the most profound sentences in the entire Bible. Perhaps its fullest meaning could never be completely explained. It reveals a part of the character of God. The construction of the Greek does not completely equate love with God. In other words, you couldn't say, "love is God." Love does not completely describe God, but God completely defines love. He is love. His nature is loving, and love can never be absent from His being or any of His actions.

In verses 9–10 John told how we know what God's love is and how great that love is. We know what it is because it was shown or revealed to us in the sending of Jesus (v. 9a). Love was first seen in Jesus' self-sacrifice (3:16); now it is seen in God's sending of His Son.

The greatness of this love is described by John in four ways. First, it is seen in the value of God's gift (v. 9b). Not only was the gift in the person of Jesus, God's Son, but He was His "one and only" (*monogenes*) Son. His uniqueness made the gift valuable. Second, the greatness of the

It is important to remember that the heresy invading the churches in and around Ephesus claimed much authority due to their special *gnosis* or knowledge. The statement that they "do not know God" would not only be true, but would be quite offensive to such an arrogant group of false teachers.

How can a loving God allow this to happen? or, *If God is love, how can He send people to hell?* These questions are often asked. Job asked similar questions. God is big enough to handle these questions. As with Job, God will bring to clarity what initially was puzzling. We will come to acknowledge that all of God's actions are loving. When our understanding of love seems to conflict with what we see God doing, we should bring our concerns to God and wait before Him for light.

"For God so loved the world that he gave his one and only Son, that whoever believes in him shall not perish but have eternal life. For God did not send his Son into the world to condemn the world, but to save the world through him" (John 3:16–17).

gift is seen in the purpose of the Son's mission: "That we might live through him" (v. 9c). Third, it is seen in the condition of the recipients of His love. We were not worthy and were completely undeserving ("not that we loved God," v. 10a); yet, His love was great enough that He still sent His Son for us. Fourth, it is seen in the manner in which the gift ultimately had to be given: "As an atoning sacrifice for our sins" (v. 10b). In order for us to "live through him," He not only had to come, but He had to die (see commentary at 2:2 for explanation of "atoning"). This truly is a "great" love.

■ *John appealed to his readers to love one*
■ *another because authentic Christians are*
■ *people who love others in the way that God*
■ *loves them.*

The Obligation to Love (4:11)

After giving the appeal to love and reflecting on the love of God, John now returned to the appeal by way of our obligation. The call to love one another is now mentioned as a factual obligation. The key word is "ought" (Greek *opheilomen*, used in 2:6; 3:16). It is a strong word describing a moral obligation. After seeing the love of God in the gift of Christ, it is not that we "ought" to love others in the sense that we "should" do it. It is that we are bound and obligated to love others in the same self-sacrificing way.

It is good for Christians to remind themselves of God's gift by way of prayer, reading, telling, and listening to the story of Christ's incarnation and death. The story of the "old rugged cross" should never be allowed to grow cold in our lives. We should rekindle our humility and appreciation often so that we will feel the obligation to love others and to share His love with them. But whether we feel it or not, we are obligated to do so.

The Substance of the Test of Love (4:12)

John abruptly made a big statement: "No one has ever seen God." The truth of this statement is revealed throughout the Bible.

A Concluding Call to Love (4:7–12)

John went on to make an even more incredible statement. He said that the invisible God "lives in us" if we love one another. Love is not the condition for which God is waiting to come to us. If God lives in you, the natural outcome is love for others. Visible love is the test for the presence of the invisible God. Our loving attitude, and action, are evidence that we pass the test.

John went one step further before he ended this magnificent paragraph. Reciprocal Christian love is not only evidence of God's abiding presence, but John says it is evidence that God's love is being completed in us. "In us" can mean in each individual believer or in mutual Christian relationships. Both are probably true. In some indescribable manner, God is making His love perfect in us as we reflect His love to others. His love is brought to its proper end in us when we are busy loving others.

Even in Moses' close encounter with God, he could not see God visibly. "And the LORD said, 'I will cause all my goodness to pass in front of you, and I will proclaim my name, the LORD, in your presence. I will have mercy on whom I will have mercy, and I will have compassion on whom I will have compassion. But,' he said, 'you cannot see my face, for no one may see me and live'" (Exod. 33:19–20).

- *Love is the test of real relationship; and as*
- *believers, we are obligated to love others. We*
- *should be motivated by the fact that God is*
- *love, His love was demonstrated in Jesus, and*
- *His love is now being made complete in us.*

John indicated that the invisible God was revealed in Christ. "No one has ever seen God, but God the One and Only, who is at the Father's side, has made him known" (John 1:18).

QUESTIONS TO GUIDE YOUR STUDY

1. What does the phrase "God is love" (v. 8) mean?

2. How would you explain to a new Christian that we have a social obligation to love everyone?

3. What do you think John meant when he said God's love is made "complete in us" (v. 12)?

A COMBINING OF THE TESTS OF BELIEF AND LOVE (4:13–21)

The two concluding statements in verse 12 are now picked up and elaborated in the following section. While combining the tests of belief and love, John discussed further the indwelling of God (vv. 13–16) and the perfecting of God's love within the true believer (vv. 17–21).

The Indwelling of God (4:13–16)

Three different times in this paragraph John mentioned the mutual indwelling of the true believer and God (vv. 13, 15, 16). Each time he gave the evidence of this mutual indwelling. We can check on ourselves by looking for these three kinds of evidence.

The word *trinity* is never mentioned in the New Testament. There is much debate as to when the doctrine of the three-in-oneness of God actually developed, and some believe it is not a biblical concept. However, it seems quite clear that John accepted this doctrine and understood it well enough to feel he didn't need to explain it. For example, here we have all three members of the Godhead interrelated. The Father sends both the Spirit and Jesus. They are distinct, but they are all God.

The first statement of God's indwelling occurs in verse 13 and the evidence is "because he has given us his Spirit." How is this evidence? We can't see His Spirit, but we can see the evidence or fruit of His Spirit. In fact, the following two evidences (in vv. 15–16) are built upon this one. We cannot believe in Christ or love one another unless the Spirit empowers us to do so (see 1 Cor. 12:3; Gal. 5:22; 1 John 3:23–24; 4:1–3). If a person has confessed Christ and loves other people, then the Spirit is in him. And if the Spirit is in him, then God also is indwelling him. Furthermore, the Spirit Himself will bear witness to us that we belong to Him (Rom. 8:16).

In verse 14 John gave the apostolic testimony to the Son's saving mission. The "we" refers to John and the other apostles, demonstrating how faith in Christ is based on the testimony of firsthand witnesses of Christ. Their testimony is that the world is in need of salvation, the Son came as the Savior, and the Father sent Him.

The grounds for John's three tests are found in this concise statement of the gospel. He has not arbitrarily chosen the tests. As John Stott writes, "Within this statement of the gospel all three of the apostle's tests are implicitly contained, the doctrinal (it was his Son himself whom the Father sent), the social (God's love seen in the sending of his Son, 9–10, 16, obligates us to love each other), and the ethical (if Christ came to be our Saviour, we must forsake the sins from which he came to save us)" (John Stott, *The Letters of John*).

The test for assurance is now given. It is the doctrinal test. The statement, "If anyone acknowledges that Jesus is the Son of God," is the condition. To "acknowledge" means a public confession (as in 4:2). This, however, does not simply mean to recite the phrase. It is to say what a person truly believes and has accepted as true. The aorist tense refers to a single and decisive act. The only way a person can understand and have the courage to make the confession is if the Spirit prompts him to do so (4:2). Therefore, this is a valid and necessary test for the assurance that "God lives in him and he in God."

John again gave his testimony in verse 16 before he brought the test of true life. John testified that he knew and relied on God's love. But, since "God is love," the evidence that a person is in God and God in him is the character of God being lived out in his or her life. Loving attitudes and actions as well as right beliefs prove that God is living in a person.

■ *There is evidence which demonstrates the*
■ *mutual indwelling of God and the true believer.*
■ *If this evidence is seen, assurance is real.*

The Perfecting of Love (4:17–21)

John ended verse 12 with the affirmation that if we love one another, God dwells in us and His love is perfected in us. The idea of God's indwelling was expanded in verses 13–16. Now John elaborated on the idea of the perfecting of love. Previously it was God's love that was the topic, here it is our love that is perfected (v. 17). John described the results of our perfected love: confidence in the day of judgment (vv. 17b–18) and love for other Christians (vv. 19–21).

First, perfected love results in confidence when Christ returns in judgment. The word *confidence* (*parresia*) was previously used to describe the unshakable confidence we should have at Christ's Second Coming (2:28) and during our prayers (3:21). Here it is used to explain the inner assurance of the true believer to face the judgment. There can be confidence because the true believer is in the same position as Christ ("like him," v. 17c), both a child of God and the object of His love. This confidence is a sign that our love is perfected

John stated this same truth negatively in verse 18. Whereas true love toward God (due to a true relationship with God) produces confidence, a lack of love (due to a lack of relationship) produces fear. Fear or terror is the opposite of confidence. They are mutually exclusive. As John stated, "perfect love drives out fear." Fear is present when there is no saving relationship because the judgment will result in punishment. Love is perfected when there is no trace of fear at all.

Second, perfected love results in love for others (vv. 19–21). God "first loved us" (v. 19). Because of that, we love as well. God takes the initiative. We respond to His love not only in our heads but in our hearts and with our hands.

Genuine Christian love is not only expressed toward God, but it goes out to our brothers as well. While perfect love casts out fear, it also dispels hatred. As John stated earlier, a person cannot be in the light and hate his brother (2:9); neither can he claim to love God and hate his brother (4:20). That person "is a liar."

John concluded by giving two reasons why love for God results in love for others. First, it is a logical conclusion. If we can't love the people we see, then it is illogical to think we could love God whom we can't see. If we have God's love in us, then we will naturally give it to those closest to us. Second, it is a matter of obedience. If God's love is in us, then we will obey His commands (2:5). Jesus made the command clear—that we are to love God and our neighbors. We cannot separate the duties or be exclusive with our love.

John has now listed three types of people who are "liars." They are persons who claim to be true believers, but either walk in the darkness of disobedience (1:6; 2:4), deny the deity of Jesus (2:22–23), and/or hate their brother (4:20). All liars, when faced with the truth, lose their confidence. A day is coming when all masks will be dropped and all tests will be final. Shouldn't we make decisions that will lead to confidence in the end and not the revelation of our lies?

■ *Authentic Christian love is a perfecting love*
■ *that results in confidence to face the judg-*
■ *ment and loving action toward others.*

QUESTIONS TO GUIDE YOUR STUDY

1. Why did John choose these three specific tests?

2. What is the evidence of the believer and God's mutual indwelling?

3. What are the results of perfected love? How are these played out in a person's life?

THE RELATIONSHIP BETWEEN THE THREE TESTS (5:1–5)

First John 5:1–5 is difficult to outline, like most of this letter. The relationship between the three tests is described in such a way that it is difficult to unravel. Perhaps the three tests are so closely related that it is impossible to place them together in a specific order and to unpack these verses cleanly. The complexity of the argument reveals the inherent unity of the tests.

John concluded his discussion of the three tests (moral, social, and doctrinal) by affirming that it is important for the true believer to demonstrate all three signs of the presence of authentic Christianity (right actions, love, and belief). He showed how the three tests are closely related and intricately interwoven into an essential unity. All three are present in a true believer, and none can be missing in an authentic Christian.

John began with a universal principle relating to the doctrinal test of belief: "Everyone who believes that Jesus is the Christ is born of God" (5:1). The substance of the belief is acceptance that Jesus the man is Christ the divine Son who became incarnate. The tenses of the verbs are important as well. "Believes" is present tense, signifying a present and ongoing belief. "Is born" is perfect tense, meaning "has been born in the past and the results remain." Ongoing belief is the result of the new birth—not the cause of it.

This new birth that brings about our believing also involves our loving. To be given birth by God naturally leads to loving God. "Everyone who loves the father loves his child as well" (v. 1b). John applied a social proverb to the Christian family. Love for a parent carries with it love for the parent's children as well. Anyone who loves God must also love God's children.

Verse 2 shows the relationship between love for others and love for God as well as obedience to God. Authentic love for others is grounded in love for and obedience to God. Love and obedience are so related that obedience defines love. John wrote, "This is love for God: to obey his commands" (v. 3a). John also added that "his commands are not burdensome" (v. 3b). Love is practical and leads to obedient actions—actions which are not difficult to fulfill.

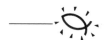

Jesus stated, "Come to me, all you who are weary and burdened, and I will give you rest. Take my yoke upon you and learn from me, for I am gentle and humble in heart, and you will find rest for your souls. For my yoke is easy and my burden is light" (Matt. 11:28–30).

Right belief, right actions, right love—all of these sound burdensome. How can John claim they are not? He quickly gives the answer: "For everyone born of God overcomes the world" (v. 4a). The new birth provides the power continually to win victory over the world and its evil powers. The burden of obedience is lifted because the power of victory is inherent within the new birth.

John referred to victory over the world two more times. In verse 4b the verb points to a definite act. It is probably referring to their past victory over the false teachers. What was it that helped bring the victory over the heretics? It was not their new birth specifically, but their belief, "even our faith" (v. 4c). The last occurrence is with a present tense (v. 5), as was the first one (v. 4a), signaling the present and ongoing victory. The person who has such a daily victory is the one who believes correctly that "Jesus is the Son of God."

■ *The argument has gone full circle, and each of*
■ *the three tests have been related to one another.*
■ *Authentic Christians are those who believe cor-*
■ *rectly who Jesus is, and who are born of God.*
■ *They love both the Father and His children and*
■ *also keep His commands. They are able to keep*
■ *His commands because they overcome the*
■ *world. They overcome the world because they*
■ *believe correctly and are, therefore, born of*
■ *God. Remove any of these evidences and one*
■ *fails the test. Fail one test and enough proof is*
■ *gathered to pronounce the verdict that the one*
■ *being tested is not authentic. The true believer*
■ *will see all the evidence in some degree in his or*
■ *her life, while perfection will not occur until the*
■ *end of time.*

QUESTIONS TO GUIDE YOUR STUDY

1. Will all believers pass all three of the tests John presented?

2. How are John's three tests interrelated?

THE TESTIMONIES FOR OUR ASSURANCE (5:6–17)

After John began and ended his last paragraph with the aspect of faith in Jesus, the natural question arises: How can a person come to faith in Jesus as the Son of God? John answered the question by claiming that faith is dependent on having the right kind of witnesses. In this section of John's letter, he explained that idea by first presenting the three witnesses (vv. 6–9), the results due to their testimonies (vv. 10–12), and finally our resulting assurances (vv. 13–17).

THE THREE TESTIMONIES (5:6–9)

In verses 6–9 John presented three different witnesses who testifed that Jesus is in fact the Christ. The first witness is the "water." The second witness is the "blood." The third witness is the "Spirit."

Various interpretations have been given as to the identity of the first two witnesses: "water and blood." They generally break down into three different lines of thought: (1) they refer to baptism and the Lord's Supper; (2) they are symbolic references to the water and blood that flowed from Jesus' side at His death as a result of the spear thrust (John 19:34–35); and (3) "water" refers to His baptism, and "blood" refers to His death.

The third interpretation seems to be the best, although John could be using these as terms with one primary meaning along with other shades of meaning. Blood would be an unprecedented symbol for the Lord's Supper as well as the object that it is pointing to as a sign. Furthermore, it is difficult to see how John could say Jesus "came" (aorist) through the ordinances. In the same way it is difficult to see how Jesus "came" through the water and blood at His death when they actually flowed out of Him.

Baptism and death is the best interpretation for the meaning of "water and blood." God voiced His approval of Jesus at His baptism (Matt. 3:16–17). He also voiced it again before Jesus' death (John 12:27–30). Water and blood seem to be unique and strange words to represent these events, but they must have been understood by John's readers because he didn't

"As soon as Jesus was baptized, he went up out of the water. At that moment heaven was opened, and he saw the spirit of God descending like a dove and lighting on him. And a voice from heaven said, 'This is my Son, whom I love; with him I am well pleased" (Matt. 3:16–17). "Now my heart is troubled, and what shall I say? 'Father, save me from this hour'? No, it was for this very reason I came to this hour, Father, glorify your name!' Then a voice came from heaven, 'I have glorified it, and will glorify it again.' The crowd that was there and heard it said it had thundered; others said an angel had spoken to him. Jesus said, 'This voice was for your benefit, not mine'" (John 12:27–30).

This is not a technical or insignificant detail. Anyone who does not accept that Jesus was and is always the Christ will have a confused doctrine of salvation. If the divine Son of God did not take both our nature and our sins upon Him, then He has no effect in our reconciliation to God. Any church, person, or religious organization that teaches such false doctrine should be refuted and avoided.

"Therefore I tell you that no one who is speaking by the Spirit of God says, 'Jesus be cursed; and no one can say, 'Jesus is Lord,' except by the Holy Spirit" (1 Cor. 12:3).

explain them. If they do represent baptism and death, then John presented an objective witness to both the beginning and ending of Jesus' earthly mission.

By referring to the water and the blood (Jesus' baptism and death) as witnesses, John gave a valid testimony for establishing faith as well as refuting the false teachers. Gnosticism taught that Jesus was born a man and died a man, that the Christ came upon Him at His baptism and left Him before His death. John refuted this teaching when he claimed, "He did not come by water only, but by water and blood" (v. 6b). In other words, He is Jesus Christ—the man who was simultaneously the Christ at both His baptism and in His death, as He always was and will be just one person.

The third witness is the Spirit. The content of John's testimony is not mentioned, but the context of the letter as well as John's Gospel indicate that it must have been a testimony about Christ (4:2; John 15:26). John indicated the Spirit testifies because He "is the truth" (v. 6c) and, therefore, is trustworthy. John must have referred to the inner testimony of the Holy Spirit (2:20, 27; 4:1–6; 1 Cor. 12:3), and he may have included as well the total witness of the Spirit (including that at Jesus' baptism, and Pentecost).

John went on to establish the validity of these three witnesses. First, he claimed the witnesses are in agreement in their testimonies (vv. 7–8). The law required the collaboration of two or three witnesses before a testimony was considered admissible (Deut. 19:15; cf. John 8:17–18). John showed that the testimonies describing who Jesus is meets even these requirements. Second, John gave both objective (baptism and death) and subjective (the Spirit's inner testimony) witnesses. Finally, the testimonies are valid because they are the testimonies that God Himself, through these three vessels, "has given about his Son" (v. 9, perfect tense indicating continuing validity).

- *The three witnesses that testify about Jesus*
- *are the water, the blood, and the Spirit. Each*
- *assists the believer toward salvation.*

THE RESULTS FROM THE TESTIMONIES (5:10–12)

There are two different types of responses to the testimonies about Christ. One response is to believe in the Son of God (v. 10a). This is described by John as being synonymous with accepting the testimony of God about Christ (v. 9). The other is not to "believe God" (v. 10b), which is the same as not believing in the Son and not accepting the testimony of God. To believe means to rely upon, to trust in, or to commit to the Son of God. Not to believe is to not make such commitments.

The result from not believing is simply stated by John: "Anyone who does not believe God has made him out to be a liar" (v. 10b). As in 1:10, this does not mean it shows God to be a liar; rather, it means that the unbeliever is accusing God of a lie. Therefore, unbelief is not simply a lack of faith, but it is a deplorable sin. The unbeliever hears the true testimonies of God and tags them false, thereby rejecting Christ, accusing God of lying, and forsaking salvation ("does not have life," v. 12b).

If you compare the texts of the NIV and the KJV, you will see that there is a difference in verses 7–8. The NIV reveals the original text, and the KJV "addition" is not found in any Greek manuscript prior to the fourth century. The added text provides an explicit reference to the Trinity and holds emotional value to some people. Through pressure, Erasmus included the text in his 1522 Greek New Testament (though he was sure it was not original). From there it found its way into the King James Bible. Most current textual critics are in agreement that the variant is not original. Bruce Metzger writes, "That these words are spurious and have no right to stand in the New Testament is certain" (Bruce Metzger, *A Textual Commentary on the Greek New Testament*, 3d. ed., United Bible Societies, 1975, pg. 715).

There comes a time for the lost person to believe in Jesus Christ. When people hear God's Word, understand, and reject Him anyway, they have made a bad decision. The results of this decision continue to linger in their lives until they change their unbelieving hearts. The perfect tenses of the verbs in "has made him out to be a liar because he has not believed" (v. 10), describe a continuing result of a past decision. As B. F. Westcott wrote, "When the crisis of choice came he refused the message: he made God a liar: he did not believe on His testimony: and the result of that decision entered into him and clings to him" (B. F. Westcott, *The Epistles of St. John*, 187). The moment of conviction by God, the moment of the slightest revelation of light, should prompt the lost person to an immediate response.

John continued to discuss the results that come to the believer. The first result is that "this testimony" is "in his heart" (v. 10a). In other words, he is given a deeper and inner assurance of his salvation by the testimony of the Spirit. It is the historical testimony of "water and blood" and the objective/subjective testimony of the Holy Spirit that leads to belief, but, also, it is the deeper subjective testimony of the Spirit that results from belief.

The second result for the believer is the assurance of eternal life. The "testimony" of verse 11 is now the deeper testimony of the Spirit that comes as a result of belief. The Spirit assures the believer of his "eternal life." This is John's special term that encompasses salvation, the Kingdom of God, and relationship with Christ. It includes eternity in time, but it is much more than that. Before John restated the two different resulting conditions of the believers and the unbelievers, he claimed that the Spirit assures the believer of this grand result of faith—eternal life.

- *The three testimonies produce in a person*
- *either salvation or rejection of God. If a per-*
- *son is a believer, then these testimonies result*
- *in a deeper assurance and understanding of*
- *eternal life.*

OUR RESULTING ASSURANCE (5:13–17)

John quickly headed toward his conclusion by adding some final words of assurance to end this section of his letter. He spoke again about the assurance of eternal life (v. 13) and confidence in prayer (vv. 14–17). These two main thoughts concluded his section about the three witnesses and our assurance.

Verse 13 contains another of John's purpose statements for the writing of this letter. Perhaps this one serves as the primary purpose. He wanted the true believers he was writing to "know" that they had eternal life. He delivered to them some accurate but strong criteria to test their relationship with Christ, but his purpose was to instill assurance into those who knew Christ.

John discussed another assurance of believers in verses 14–17. They can be assured that God will answer their prayers: "We know that we have what we asked of him" (v. 15b). He began by claiming that they have "confidence" (*parresia*, same as in 2:28; 3:21; 4:17) that God hears our prayers: "If we ask anything according to his will" (v. 14). The idea of "hearing" probably means that God listens to and answers our prayers. It is not an unqualified promise of answered prayer. The condition of answered prayer in 3:22 was living in God's will—here it is praying in God's will. This is the inclusive statement on the conditions of effectual prayer in the New Testament. The promise is a present granting of the request.

Before John closed his thoughts on prayer, he gave a specific example of the efficacy of intercessory prayer (vv. 16–17). The example John chose was when "anyone sees his brother commit a sin that does not lead to death" (v. 16a). These verses have a few interpretative knots that are seen in this statement. First, who is the "brother"? Although some interpreters think this refers to people or neighbors in general, it is probably another instance of

In 5:6–12, John spoke in detail about what he said briefly in his Gospel. John clearly stated his purpose for writing the Fourth Gospel. In speaking of all he wrote, he stated, "But these are written that you may believe that Jesus is the Christ, the Son of God, and that by believing you may have life in his name" (John 20:31). Life comes by believing, and believing comes from a testimony about Christ. In John 21:24, John spoke about himself and called what he was doing in the Gospel a testimony: "This is the disciple who testifies to these things, and who wrote them down. We know that his testimony is true."

Throughout the writings of John, you can trace four basic stages in the lives of Christians: a witness is given to them, they believe, they receive eternal life, and they gain assurance in their status of eternal life. John wrote his Gospel to bear witness so people might believe and receive eternal life. He wrote this letter to shore up their hearts toward assurance.

Some people think that holding some degree of doubt about your salvation and future life in heaven is a sign of righteous humility. This is not so. God's desire, according to His revealed will (5:13), is that His children will know without doubt that they have eternal life.

John's teaching on prayer in 5:14–15 is one of the most important ones in the New Testament. Several lessons can be learned. First, the promise of answered prayer is for the believer. Second, prayer is not a magic formula; God is not a personal genie. Third, we should be glad God does it this way. It would be a messed-up world and we would live messed-up lives if God simply gave us everything we wanted. His will is best. Pray to find it.

John's technical use of the term referring to fellow Christians in their community (2:9–11; 3:10, 13–17; 4:20–21).

Second, what is the "sin that leads to death"? Volumes have been written on this subject, and opinions are varied. The main options are: (1) a specific act of sin, such as murder, adultery, intentional sins, and so on; (2) a lifestyle of sin; (3) apostasy, or total renunciation of Christ and faith; or (4) blasphemy against the Holy Spirit.

John's readers must have known exactly what he was talking about, or at least he seems to have assumed they did. This thought is simply a parenthetical idea. John's main point is that prayer asked in accordance with God's will, will be answered. The "sin that leads to death" is an example that his readers would have understood.

The best solution is perhaps found in the historical context. The Gnostic opponents had willfully and vigorously rejected the Spirit's witness to the work and person of Christ. The "sin that leads to death" must have been a reference to their denial of the truth. This seems to be the best solution. The "brother" (discussed above) may be a reference to someone who appears to be a brother but whose sin will reveal otherwise. Whatever the solution, the idea John communicated is that it is a type of sinning that leads to spiritual death.

In John's example, he pointed out that if you see a brother sinning in a way other than in a sin that leads to death, you should pray for him (v. 16a). It is through these kinds of prayer that the sinning person will gain eternal life. This illustrates John's earlier point. Prayer in accordance with God's will results in God's answers.

Verse 17 simply serves as a clarification. Just in case people get the wrong idea about sinful deeds since John mentioned two different "classes" of sins, he reminds the readers that all sin is wrong and no sin is trivial. Earlier he said, "sin is lawlessness" (3:4). Now he indicated it is "wrongdoing." All activities against the law or justice are sin, and all sin is serious.

- *John concluded this section and readied his*
- *readers for the conclusion by reminding*
- *them of the assurance and confidence that*
- *comes when a person accepts the validity of*
- *the three witnesses and believes in Jesus*

QUESTIONS TO GUIDE YOUR STUDY

1. What are the three witnesses and how do they bear witness to Jesus?
2. How can a lack of belief be considered sin?
3. What did John mean by the "sin that leads to death"?

The "unpardonable sin" was considered blaspheming the Holy Spirit. In the context of the Gospels, this sin was attributing to Satan the work done by Christ. Jesus said, "'He who is not with me is against me, and he who does not gather with me scatters. And so I tell you, every sin and blasphemy will be forgiven men, but the blasphemy against the Spirit will not be forgiven'" (Matt. 12:30–31). "'But whoever blasphemes against the Holy Spirit will never be forgiven; he is guilty of an eternal sin.' He said this because they were saying, 'He has an evil spirit'" (Mark 3:29–30).

THREE CERTAINTIES AND A CHARGE (5:18–21)

John concluded his first letter by reminding and challenging his readers. He concisely stated three certainties that a believer can have (vv. 18–20) before he concluded with one quick but solemn charge (v. 21).

THE THREE CERTAINTIES (5:18–20)

John used three rapid fire "we know" statements (vv. 18, 19, 20) to rally his final thoughts.

John's definitions of sin go against the standards of right and wrong held by pop culture today. John clearly declared there is a standard of right and wrong, although the culture maintains that right and wrong are individual matters. To be a Christian is to be in the world, but not to live by the world's standards. Jesus said, "'If you hold to my teaching, you are really my disciples. Then you will know the truth, and the truth will set you free'" (John 8:31b–32).

The Psalmist recorded God's desires of protection for His people. The statement in 1 John 5:18 may be an allusion to Ps. 105:15: "Do not touch my anointed ones; do my prophets no harm."

First, John states that we know the true believer does not live a lifestyle of sin (v. 18a). There may be acts of sin in the true believer's life, but there the old life of sin will not be present. This is a general statement about all believers.

Two reasons are given for this (v. 18b). One, because Christ ("the one who was born of God") "keeps him safe." Christ watches over the Christian and protects. It is not the believer who is able to overcome Satan and his ways; it is up to Christ to do the protecting. Two, the believer doesn't continue to sin because the "evil one cannot touch him." To "touch" doesn't mean to engage or feel, but "to grasp." Satan may assault or attack, but he cannot lay hold of us enough to defeat us because Christ is on guard.

Second, John stated that we know something about John and his readers and something about the world (v. 19). John included himself when he wrote, "We are children of God." They had assurance of their salvation in the family of God. They had truly been born of Him. The world, on the other hand, "is under the control of the evil one." The evil one, Satan himself, has the people of the world and the evil powers in the world under his control.

Third, John stated that we know that Jesus has both come and given us understanding (v. 20). This is his last and most foundational statement of the three. It includes the acknowledgment of Jesus being the "Son of God" (v. 19a) as well as God's "Son Jesus Christ" (v. 19b). The statement reconfirms both the historical ("has come") and experiential ("has given") knowledge which He has brought. The purpose of His coming is so that we may know (relationally) the True One, which in fact the readers do ("we are in him who is true," v. 19b). The True One is God, and the experiential understanding of our relationship with Him is mediated through "his Son Jesus Christ."

The final statement ("He is the true God and eternal life") is probably a reference to God. It could refer to Jesus. If so, it would be the most clear statement to the deity of Jesus in the New Testament. However, it is best to see it as another reference to the "true one." As such, God is defined as both the only "real" God and "eternal life."

The Greek word translated "is under the control" in verse 19 is *keitai*. It literally means "to lie." It paints a sad but true picture of the state of the world. Satan has it, and it lies helplessly in his power. The word portrays the world as a calm and almost sleeping victim that does not even struggle to get loose.

■ *John moved toward the conclusion of his let-*
■ *ter by claiming three certainties: (1) true*
■ *believers do not live sinful lifestyles, (2) the*
■ *readers are true believers, and (3) Jesus is*
■ *the incarnated Christ. If all this is truly and*
■ *factually known, salvation is a sure thing.*

THE CHARGE (5:21)

John closed his letter not with a formal closing, but with a gentle address of affection and a concise charge. Identifying his readers again as his "dear children," he tenderly charged them to "keep yourselves from idols." To "keep" means "to guard."

This entire letter is a detailed delineation of what a true believer is and does. Moral obedience, genuine love, and right beliefs are the marks of a Christian. Anything else is incongruent with our Father's character and our new nature. Now, with the image of the true God and His divine Son in the foreground and the false teachers and their heresy in the background, John summarized the true believers important responsibility by charging them to worship nothing other than God.

QUESTIONS TO GUIDE YOUR STUDY

1. What are the three certainties listed by John in this section?
2. How do you think God keeps His children safe from Satan?
3. Why do you think John ended his letter with a command and not a normal salutation?

INTRODUCTION TO 2 & 3 JOHN

The short length of both 2 and 3 John, as well as the relative neglect of these books by the early church, add to their interest. These are the two shortest books in the New Testament, each containing less than 250 Greek words. Many of the themes discussed in detail in 1 John appear in these letters. A look at the issues of authorship, recipients, date, purpose, and structure will assist in understanding these letters. These issues will be discussed for both letters before the commentary is given on 2 and 3 John separately.

AUTHORSHIP OF 2 AND 3 JOHN

The external evidence for authorship of both of these letters is much less than for 1 John. Their canonicity was questioned in the early period of church history, as they were listed among the "disputed letters." However, no early Christian writer attributed the authorship of 2 and 3 John to anyone other than the apostle John.

The internal evidence lends support to Johannine authorship. Both the vocabulary and general themes of the letters are similar to 1 John. For example, the reality of Christ "having come in the flesh" (1 John 4:2; 2 John 7) and the importance of obedience to verify that one is a child of God (1 John 3:10; 3 John 11) are also important in these letters.

The author identified himself in both of these letters with the phrase "the elder" (*presbuteros*, 2 John 1, 3 John 1). Although this can lend support to John as the author, it has also been the point of much debate against Johannine authorship. Yet, this would not be the first time that an apostle referred to himself as an elder (1 Pet. 5:1). It was probably John's way of referring to his advanced age as well as his authoritative position among the churches of Ephesus.

RECIPIENTS AND ORIGINATION OF 2 AND 3 JOHN

In both letters a recipient is named. In 2 John the letter is written to "the chosen lady and her children" (v. 1). Again, who this refers to specifically is uncertain. Some scholars view this as a title of a personal friend of John's. Others see it as a personification designating a local congregation of believers. The latter seems the best interpretation for several reasons: the language of love and the command given to love in verse 5 seems inappropriate for an individual; there are no explicit personal references such as those found in 3 John; the writer switches between "you" singular and "you" plural often in the letter (unobservable in most modern translations) while being consistent with the singular in 3 John; and it was normal to personify towns or institutions in the first century much as we do today.

The third letter of John was written to "Gaius" (v. 1). He appears to have been a leading member of

Peter the apostle, wrote, "To the elders among you, I appeal as a fellow elder, a witness of Christ's sufferings and one who also will share in the glory to be revealed" (1 Pet. 5:1).

Thanks to the expansion and economic developments of the Roman Empire during the first century, travel had become much easier than ever before. The Romans had established a fine network of roads that connected most of the empire. The *Pax Romana* (peace of Rome) made traveling safer, and the spread of Greek and Latin as universal languages made it more inviting. All of these changes helped the spread of Christianity during the first century.

a local church. Exactly where Gaius lived is unknown, but it was probably around Ephesus, where John continued to live and write these two letters.

DATE OF THE WRITING OF 2 AND 3 JOHN

The data for a solid conviction on the date of the writing of either of these letters is vague. Again, as with 1 John, it appears best to place them after John's Gospel because of content. How they related to 1 John is difficult to determine. It appears best to see them as written after 1 John, possibly even sent together with it in a bundle. The referral to "the antichrist" in 2 John 7 without a more detailed discussion (see 1 John 2:18–23) seems to suggest this followed that letter in time. These were probably written shortly after 1 John or at the same time as 1 John (ca. A.D. 85–95).

THE PURPOSES OF 2 AND 3 JOHN

John did not explicitly state a purpose in either of these two letters as he did in his Gospel and in his first letter. However, it appears that 2 John was written to warn against showing hospitality to false teachers (v. 10). This would have assisted the spread of errant doctrine. Intertwined in this discussion is John's teaching of the correct doctrines and actions of true believers.

Third John appears to be John's effort to confront a church problem by encouraging Gaius (vv. 2–8) and Demetrius (v. 12), discussing the problems caused by Diotrephes (vv. 9–11), and setting up an upcoming personal visit (vv. 13–14). Diotrephes had not welcomed the itinerant Christian teachers with the proper hospitality and had discouraged others from doing so. Therefore, 2 John and 3 John have the same background and similar purposes. Second John

As both Christian people and itinerant Christian teachers traveled, they would need a place to stay. Inns and hotels as we know them today were nonexistent in the first century. The ancient inns were not as comfortable as a private home. They usually housed as many fleas and as much dust as they did guests. They were also generally known for their dishonorable atmosphere, which was prompted by the poor character of most innkeepers. So it became a common practice for local Christians to open their homes to traveling Christians. Such hospitality is seen throughout the New Testament (Acts 16:15; 17:7; 21:8, 16; Rom. 16:23). This genuine hospitality was also abused by people who were simply looking for free lodging.

is more negative and 3 John is more positive on the issue of Christian hospitality.

THE STRUCTURE OF 2 AND 3 JOHN

The structure of both of these letters is quite simple. They both contain the elements of a traditional first-century letter (except 3 John omits a formal greeting). Each letter would probably fit on a single sheet of papyrus as a normal letter. Each has a simple outline as follows:

- *Second and 3 John were both written by the*
- *apostle John to a local church and a church*
- *leader, respectively, shortly after 1 John was*
- *written (ca. A.D. 85–95). Second John was*
- *written to warn against showing hospitality*
- *to false teachers, and 3 John was written to*
- *encourage proper hospitality to Christian*
- *teachers.*

INTRODUCTION TO 2 JOHN (VV. 1–3)

John's introduction to this letter is in the typical pattern of ancient letters. He mentioned the sender and the recipients and gave a greeting. John identified himself as "the elder" (v. 1). This could be an official title or simply a designation of his age. The "chosen lady and her children" are the addressees of the letter. This was John's way of addressing a specific church and its members.

After mentioning the recipients, John gave a long qualification about the church ("whom" of

The term *elder* could have been an official title of John. While some see a distinction between elder (*presbuteros*), bishop/overseer (*episcopos*), and pastor/shepherd (*poimen*), the New Testament uses these titles interchangeably for the leaders of a local church. For example, Paul referred to the same people by all three names: "From Miletus, Paul sent to Ephesus for the elders of the church . . . 'Keep watch over yourselves and all the flock of which the Holy Spirit has made you overseers. Be shepherds of the church of God, which he bought with his own blood'" (Acts 20:17, 28). The same thing occurs in 1 Peter 5:1–2.

v. 1, masculine in Greek, refers to the lady and the children). First, he said he loved them in "the truth," which means in sincerity. Second, he declared that all the believers loved this church as well. "Truth" at the end of verse 1 is the revelation of Christ in the gospel or Christ Himself. Therefore, to know this truth is to be a true believer. The love for this church was as broad as the community of faith. Finally, the reason for this love was because the truth was in them. This was not some fanciful or fickle type of love.

In John's description of the truth within them (v. 2), he struck a wonderful note of security. The truth is said to be a present, indwelling reality ("which lives in us") that will continue forever ("and will be with us forever"). The "with us" is emphatic, and drawing a strong contrast between the heretics who will leave eventually (vv. 7; 1 John 2:19) and the enduring truth within the individual that sustains the fellowship of the true community of Christ.

The greeting of this letter (v. 3) has some unique features which shed light on John's point. Any adjustments to the normal pattern of a greeting are intentional and reveal something the writer was trying to emphasize. John added "mercy" to the normal "grace and peace" formula, emphasizing salvation as well as our need of it. John also added the phrase "the Father's Son" to the customary greeting as a way of relating his familiar theme of sonship. Finally, he added the phrase "in truth and love" as a way of reiterating the characteristics of the Christian life.

■ *John opened his letter to this church with*
■ *words of encouragement. He shared with*
■ *them his love and built them up in the secu-*
■ *rity of their faith.*

PURPOSE OF 2 JOHN (vv. 4–11)

The purpose of this letter is now unfolded. John was concerned for both the fellowship of the congregation and a coming threat to the local church. He encouraged them and challenged them in their love and obedience (vv. 4–6) before he warned them and instructed them about the Antichrist (vv. 7–11).

ENCOURAGEMENT FOR FELLOWSHIP WITHIN THE CONGREGATION (2 JOHN 4–6)

John had "great joy" that he expressed to this church because he had found some of the members "walking in the truth." Either he himself had met them or he had received word about them. He rejoiced because they believed the truth and obeyed its teaching, which is what they had been commanded to do.

John next encouraged the church to heed the commands of love and obedience. The command to love was not new (*kainos*) to them; it was one they had known since the beginning of their Christian life and had been around since the Old Testament (see discussion on 1 John 2:7–11). Love and obedience are reciprocal

Church leaders should find good counsel from John's reaction. "Joy" is a natural part of ministry. Can there be any better joy than seeing people's lives changed and being conformed to the image of Christ? But his joy was the result of "some" of the church members' lives. His ministry was not 100 percent effective. The whole flock was not obediently following after Christ. He couldn't say that all the church's members were "walking in the truth." He could just say "some." Maybe we should not be surprised when we discover that every church member is not living in obedience to Christ.

duties. Love was defined by John as walking "in obedience to his commands" (v. 6a), and his command was to walk in love (v. 6b). In this brief encouragement to the church, John again alluded to the three tests in his first letter (truth/belief, love, and obedience). Here he celebrated their faithfulness to these tests and encouraged them to press on toward further application of these truths in their lives.

- *Having found members of the church living*
- *their lives faithfully, John rejoiced and*
- *pushed them forward in their duties of love*
- *and obedience.*

WARNING ABOUT A THREAT FROM OUTSIDE THE CONGREGATION (2 JOHN 7–11)

After rejoicing over and encouraging the true believers, John turned to the topic of how believers are to be related to those who are persistent in wrong behavior and on believing sound doctrine. Though "some" (v. 4) were walking in the truth, he warned about the "many" (v. 7) who were opposed to the truth. In verse 7 he described these "deceivers" before issuing two warnings to the church (vv. 8–9 and 10–11).

John warned about the "deceivers" of the church as opposed to the children of the church. The deceivers were out to lead others astray, to cause them to drift away from the truth. They should be seen as identical with the "false prophets" and "antichrists" of 1 John 2:18–19; 4:1. Their having "gone out into the

It is helpful to note how John encouraged and led this church. The use of the proper personal pronouns in our discussions with other church members is crucial. John included himself in the commands by using "we." Although he was the elder, it is as if he stepped from behind the pulpit, sat in the pew with his people, and said "Now here is what we must do." A leader should follow his or her own teaching.

The Christians were not the only traveling teachers in the first-century world. Many devoted followers of various religions hit the roads to extol their beliefs and win a material profit at the same time. Such schemes were not always easily detectable. The question of whom to host was a practical concern for these believers.

world" is a reference probably to their leaving the church as well as their mission to teach lies.

These false teachers' most recognizable characteristic was their rejection of the incarnation of Christ. John did not say that they taught against the truth of the incarnation of Jesus, but that they "do not acknowledge Jesus Christ as coming in the flesh" (v. 7). They were deceivers, and they may not have revealed their true beliefs, but their true position was to reject the Incarnation. This was a double offense. They rejected Christ and they deceived people and, therefore, each one was "the deceiver and the antichrist" (v. 7).

With the deceivers presented for who they really were, John warned the church to "watch out" for this false teaching lest they fall prey to it. This is the same warning given by Jesus in Mark 13:23. The false teachers were deceivers and so they were subtle and clever, mischievous and deceptive. A sharp eye was the true believers' best method of defense.

One reason was given for the need to "watch out." John presented it negatively and then positively: "That you do not lose what you have worked for, but that you may be rewarded fully" (v. 8b). John was surely not talking about their salvation. They did not work for that; it was a gift (see John 4:10). He referred to their reward to be given at Christ's return. John didn't want their reward to be stolen away by these false teachers. He wanted them to be "rewarded fully," so, he warned them to "watch out."

John added support to this first warning by contradicting a claim of the false teachers (v. 9). These Gnostic-type teachers claimed a superior knowledge that moved them ahead of the normal

Jesus taught about false, deceiving teachers also: "For false Christs and false prophets will appear and perform signs and miracles to deceive the elect—if that were possible. So be on your guard; I have told you everything ahead of time" (Mark 13:22–23).

Reward (*misthos*) has as its basic meaning "a workman's wages." In this passage John picked up on its common New Testament usage—a payment or honor to be received in heaven. The heavenly "reward" is never described precisely in the New Testament, although it is often held up as a motivation for doing right while we live on this earth. Paul painted the clearest picture of the reward ceremony. Both motivational and convicting, his description is found in 1 Cor. 3:8–15.

Christians. John sarcastically claimed that these false teachers had run too far. In their leaving of the true teachings about Christ, they had also left behind God. It is only the one who "continues in the teaching" who has "both the Father and the Son" (v. 9b). John taught this in his first letter (1 John 2:22–23), and reminded them here so it would help them "watch out."

Here we have some helpful hints on how to deal with members of false religions who come knocking on our doors selling their "stuff." Recognize first that the false teaching concerns the doctrine of Christ. These are not guidelines from John on how to deal with fellow Christians who have different opinions on "minor" doctrines. First, the Christian response to the person must always be given in love. Rudeness and unkindness are not the marks of a Christian. Second, the Christian response must be assertive and direct. No compromise of one's doctrinal position should be made, and no assistance or encouragement should be given in the spread of such false teachings. It is not more loving to be tolerant of such teachings. Love points people to Christ, not away from Him.

John's second warning was not about buying into the false teaching, but about assisting its distribution. The person who "comes to you" (v. 10) is one who approaches with the purpose of teaching you his ways. He is not just a person with different views who is coming for a casual visit. He is a false teacher. In fact, it may be that this is a visit to the church (since "you" is plural) which generally met in a home. However, the warning applies to both a church and a personal home.

John gives a clear command to the Christian about how to respond when a false teacher comes: "Do not take him into your house or welcome him" (v. 10). In other words, do not encourage his ways or assist him. To do so would be to further the effectiveness of the false teaching and move the teacher deeper into its errant system. John's descriptive words for this person's efforts is "wicked work" (v. 11). In order not to become an accomplice in such an evil adventure, John warned us not to encourage or assist its teacher.

- *John warned the believers to keep an eye out*
- *for the false teachers so they wouldn't get*
- *caught in their false doctrine or lose their*
- *heavenly rewards. He also instructed them*
- *not to welcome them into their homes to*
- *assist their errant mission.*

CONCLUSION OF 2 JOHN (vv. 12–13)

John closesd his second letter, but he was not finished with the conversation. He wanted to hold his remaining comments for a personal visit. "Paper and ink" seemed to be the inappropriate medium in which to continue. The reason he wanted to visit them and talk with them was "so that our joy may be complete" (v. 12). He hoped the joy that was embarked upon when he found some of their members living in the truth would be brought to completion when he united with the whole church in personal Christian fellowship.

The final sentence of the letter was John's way of sending a greeting from a fellow congregation. "Your chosen sister" (v. 13) corresponds with "the chosen lady" (v. 1). So as John came to the end of his papyrus sheet, he signed the letter and got ready to pack his bags for a visit.

Although books and papers have their place, such statements as these concluding ones by John reassure us of the value of preaching and teaching. While the communication age rushes forward with its new technologies, perhaps nothing will ever replace human-to-human, face-to-face communication for the encouragement and growth of Christians. Preaching, teaching, talking, and listening are still the best tools for encouraging spiritual growth.

QUESTIONS TO GUIDE YOUR STUDY

1. Why did John identify himself as "the elder"?

2. How do John's teachings about traveling teachers relate to our modern situation?
3. How does the concept of rewards mesh with selfless motives?
4. Is there ever a reason to show hospitality to a false teacher?

SALUTATION OF 3 JOHN (v. 1)

"Gaius" is considered by meaning to be the most common name in the Roman Empire. Several men with this name appear in the New Testament: Gaius of Ephesus, a traveling companion of Paul (Acts 19:29); Gaius of Derbe, who traveled with Paul on his last journey (Acts 20:4); and Gaius of Corinth, who was baptized by Paul (1 Cor. 1:14) and who hosted him and the church of Corinth (Rom. 16:23). There is no evidence that any of these men are the Gaius of 3 John 1.

This letter begins the same as John's second letter but immediately reveals its more personal nature. John identified himself again as "the elder" (see commentary on 2 John 1). He addressed the letter this time not to a church but to a man named "Gaius." More information about this man is not given in this letter.

Two things about Gaius are apparent from the content of the letter. First, he must have held some position in the local church. If he was not its pastor, then he was a layman with some authority. Second, he held a fond place in John's heart. John explicitly declared his love (*agape* type) for him in verse 1, and later referred to him as "dear friend" (literally "beloved") (verses 2, 5, 11). His love is "in the truth," an identical phrase to 2 John 1, and verse 4. This seems to indicate that Gaius was a person whom John had personally helped to come to know Jesus ("my children").

PRAYER AND COMMENDATION OF GAIUS (3 JOHN 2–8)

John moved into the body of his letter with a prayer for Gaius (v. 2) before he commended him for his faithfulness. He used an ancient, customary statement to pray for his good health and general success. Although these were common words found in most letters of the time, John meant them sincerely. In the midst of this polite prayer is a word of encouragement: "Even as your soul is getting along well." John did not pray for this specifically; he used Gaius's spiritual growth as a standard to pray for his physical condition. John was confident in Gaius's spiritual condition.

After the brief prayer, John commended his walk (vv. 3–4) and encouraged his Christian hospitality (vv. 5–8). Just as some of the members of the church whom John had written in 2 John had brought "great joy" to him, Gaius's personal spiritual walk had done the same (v. 3). A few fellow Christians ("some brothers") had visited Gaius's church and brought back a good report to John.

They reported two things: Gaius's continuing faithfulness to the truth in his lifestyle (v. 3b) and his love (v. 6a). These two reports combine to give a picture of a person who accepted the teachings of Christ and put them into practice through his daily behavior. For John, the "Son of Thunder" turned gentle elder, there could be "no greater joy than to hear that my children are walking in the truth" (v. 4).

In verse 5, John commended Gaius for his past love, and specifically, for his past Christian

Truth and love are key elements in spiritual maturity. As Paul wrote, "Then we will no longer be infants, tossed back and forth by the waves, and blown here and there by every wind of teaching and by the cunning and craftiness of men in their deceitful scheming. Instead, speaking the truth in love, we will in all things grow up into him who is the Head, that is, Christ. From him the whole body, joined and held together by every supporting ligament, grows and builds itself up in love, as each part does its work" (Eph. 4:14–16).

We can learn a lesson in leadership from both of John's shorter letters. Although there may be times for tough, confrontational leadership, most members of a church need encouragement in what they are doing well before their ears are attentive to what they could do better. John built up people before he broke down the problems. Perhaps most importantly, when he encouraged his people, he did not flatter them with general or unbelievable fluff. Instead, he cast light on the specific areas in which they were excelling. We need more leaders like John—well trained and equipped, excelling in character and commitment, but caring enough about the spiritual success of others that they are not afraid to be vulnerable and transparent in their conversation.

hospitality. John described him as "faithful" in what he was doing. His work matched his belief. He was true to his conviction, and this was seen in his treatment of the "brothers" who were "strangers" to him. From verse 6 we learn that these fellow Christians had come to Gaius, and he had welcomed them and allowed them to stay with him. They had reported back to John and the church about Gaius's love.

John gave instructions to Gaius for his future hospitality and then he included a general guideline for all Christian hospitality. When Gaius sends these "brothers" on their way, he should do it "in a manner worthy of God" (v. 6b). These are God's servants, traveling teachers, and they should be treated as such. John meant that they should be treated with kindness in attitude and probably in the giving of supplies.

John listed three reasons why proper hospitality should be given to these traveling Christian teachers. First, they were on a mission for Christ ("It was for the sake of the Name that they went out," v. 7a). This was an authentic Christian mission and the missionaries' motives were pure. The second reason was more practical. They would need help, but they had received no help from the non-Christian community. Because of this, John said, "we ought" ("we" is emphatic, v. 8a) to support them (though translated "hospitality" in the NIV, the Greek word *philoxenia* does not appear here). We are obligated to help our fellow Christians who are on mission for Christ. The last reason for supporting these people is "so that we may work together for the truth" (v. 8b). By showing them hospitality, we cooperate in the effort of spreading the truth and doing the truth. For all of these reasons, Gaius as well as the readers of this letter must "show hospitality to such men" (v. 8a).

- *John encouraged his friend Gaius in his*
- *Christian lifestyle. Gaius represented all*
- *John wrote about true believers in 1 John.*
- *John also instructed Gaius on the proper type*
- *of Christian hospitality that should be shown*
- *to Christian teachers.*

WARNING ABOUT DIOTREPHES (3 JOHN 9–11)

Diotrephes was some type of leader in the local church to which John wrote. He may have been the pastor. Or, perhaps he was a prominent layperson. He was the counterpart to Gaius in his character and conduct and was causing trouble in the church.

Diotrephes had rejected one of John's earlier letters to the church (v. 9a). What this letter was is unsure. It could not have been the current letter of 3 John since Diotrephes had already responded poorly to it. It could not have been 1 or 2 John because nothing is mentioned in those letters about hosting authentic missionaries. So it must have been a letter that is now lost.

Diotrephes was causing trouble by doing at least four wrong things. First, he was rejecting the authority of John (he "will have nothing to do with us," v. 9b). Second, he was spreading slanderous gossip about John ("gossiping maliciously about us," v. 10a). The Greek word for

The Greek words translated "hospitality" (*philoxenia*) or "hospitable" (*philoxenos*) are made up of two separate Greek words. *Philos* means loving, and *xenos* refers to a stranger. Therefore, the literal meaning of hospitality is "love of strangers." Neither of these words appear in this passage, but they are fleshed out in what John said about Gaius having a love for strangers and brothers (vv. 5–6a). They are found in Rom. 12:13; 1 Tim. 3:2; Tit. 1:8; Heb. 13:2; and 1 Pet. 4:9.

Notice in verses 9–10 that John switched pronouns when referring to himself. Sometimes he said "I" and sometimes he said "us." It is doubtful that he was revealing a change in who was writing the letter or in who was representing what was being said. The plural "us" is probably the plural of authority. It was John's way of referring to himself with the authority of the church.

We should be careful not to judge but to reflect. Diotrephes had fallen into a familiar trap for leaders. With the first taste of authority and recognition, a person's appetite can easily be whetted for more of each. Humility must be sought when responsibility is given.

"gossiping maliciously" means "talking nonsense," or "spreading inaccurate tales." Third, he opposed John's teaching by refusing "to welcome the brothers" (v. 10c). Fourth, he didn't show hospitality himself, and he stopped those "who want to do so and puts them out of the church" (v. 10d).

Why was Diotrephes such a troublemaker? John told us what Diotrephes's problem was. It was the sin of selfish ambition. John said Diotrephes "loves to be first" (v. 9). He had a problem with anyone being ahead of him, whether Christ, Gaius, or John. His selfish ambition apparently led to his bullying for position in the church.

John concluded his warning about Diotrephes by instructing Gaius ("dear friend") in verse 11. With the powerful and negative activity of Diotrephes being felt in the church, perhaps John was fearful that Gaius would slip into his ways. So he told him, "Do not imitate what is evil but what is good." His reason for making this statement reflects back on his moral test of his first letter. The moral activity of people reveals their spiritual condition. The person who does good is a true believer ("from God"). The one who does evil is not a believer ("has not seen God"). If John had Diotrephes in mind, he not only encouraged Gaius in his activity, but he questioned Diotrephes's spiritual condition.

- Diotrephes's selfish ambition was causing
- trouble in the local church because he was
- defying John's authority and teaching.
- Diotrephes was slandering John's character
- and trying to expel from the congregation
- those who were showing the proper Christian hospitality. John explained his errors
- and warned Gaius away from them.

COMMENDATION OF DEMETRIUS (3 JOHN 12)

As John wrote about doing good, his thoughts naturally turned away from Diotrephes and toward Demetrius. The exact identity of Demetrius and his relationship to John and the church of Gaius are not known. He may have been the person chosen to deliver the letter to its destination.

John commended Demetrius for three things. First, he had a strong reputation (he "is well spoken of by everyone"). Second, Demetrius's reputation was justified. He was "for real." Third, John gave his stamp of approval on his life. This was probably the strongest commendation that John could give, because John could say confidently to Gaius, "you know that our testimony is true."

Jesus instructed His disciples saying, "'You know that those who are regarded as rulers of the Gentiles lord it over them, and their high officials exercise authority over them. Not so with you. Instead, whoever wants to become great among you must be your servant, and whoever wants to be first must be slave of all. For even the Son of Man did not come to be served, but to serve, and to give his life as a ransom for many'" (Mark 10:42–45).

When John called Gaius to a life of imitation, he helped us see the necessity of role models. Everyone imitates someone. The key issue is how good the original is. Just as a photocopy can be no better than the original, so a person's life will be no better than whom they are trying to emulate. That is why the best "original" for the Christian is God as revealed in His Son Jesus.

In the closing words of John's letters, he used an interesting word: "friends" (*philoi*). The normal designation in the New Testament of fellow Christians was "brothers." As John closed his last personal letter to the churches of which he was "the elder," he used a striking word that Jesus used to describe His relationship with His disciples. Jesus said, "'Greater love has no one than this, that he lay down his life for his friends. You are my friends if you do what I command. I no longer call you servants, because a servant does not know his master's business. Instead, I have called you friends, for everything that I learned from my Father I have made known to you" (John 15:13–15).

CONCLUSION (3 JOHN 13–14)

The conclusion of this letter is different from that in his second letter, but there are some similarities. John had more to say, but he wanted to speak it to Gaius rather than write it. So, he concluded with his hope to come and visit soon.

Before ending his letter, John added a closing word of greeting. "Peace to you" was a common wish in many letters, but it was especially appropriate for Gaius with Diotrephes in his church. After sending the greetings from the members of his church to Gaius, John asked Gaius to greet the members of his church by name as a personal gesture of care.

QUESTIONS TO GUIDE YOUR STUDY

1. What do you know about the person to whom this letter was written? How do you know it?
2. What can you learn about dealing with rebellious people from John's treatment of Diotrephes?
3. Are there any other people named Demetrius in the Bible?
4. What did John teach about proper hospitality?

Butler, Trent C., ed. *Holman Bible Dictionary*, Nashville, Tenn.: Holman Bible Publishers, 1991.

Lea, Thomas D. *The New Testament: Its Background and Message*. Nashville, Tenn.: Broadman & Holman, 1996.

Maston, T. B. *To Walk as He Walked*, Nashville, Tenn.: Broadman Press, 1985.

Metzger, Bruce. *A Textual Commentary on the Greek New Testament: A Companion Volume to the United Bible Societies' Greek New Testament*. 3d ed. London: United Bible Societies, 1975.

Morris, Leon. *The Gospel According to John*. NICNT. Grand Rapids: Eerdmans, 1995.

Robertson, A.T. *Word Pictures in the New Testament*, vol. VI. Nashville, Tenn.: Broadman Press, 1933 (comments are from the 1960 reprint edition).

Stott, John R. W. *The Letters of John*. TNTC. Rev. ed. Grand Rapids: William B. Eerdmans Publishing Co., 1988.

Westcott, Brooke Foss. *The Epistles of St. John*. Cambridge: Macmillan and Company, 1892.

Williams, Charles B. *The New Testament in the Language of the People*. Holman Bible Publishers, 1986.